WILD WINDS

And Other Tales of Growing Up in the Outdoor West

James L. Huckabay

Featuring Paintings of Parks Reece

ISBN 0-9660761-0-9

Published by Reecer Creek Publishing, 300 North Pearl Street,
Ellensburg, WA 98926

Printed in the United States of America
by Maverick Press

Front cover painting: *Amid A Summer Night's Dream*
©1994 Parks Reece
Parks Reece's paintings used by permission of the artist.
Pencil and pen sketches by Tena Bossert, Anna Huckabay, and
Edward Bossert used by permission.
All photos by author unless otherwise credited.

ACKNOWLEDGMENTS

This book is dedicated to Brad Johnson. In July of 1988, I walked into the *Douglas County News-Press*, on the south end of the Denver Metro area, and on into his '**Editor**' office with a couple stories I'd written. I walked out a weekly columnist. We earned a little bit of Colorado Press Association recognition for some of my "Inside the Outdoors" columns, while some of the columns were probably not worth the newsprint. And, through thick and thin, Brad's friendship, coaching and faith in my writing has not wavered.

This book would not have happened without the intention, support and commitment of Keith Riexinger, publisher of *The Ellensburg Weekly.* Thank you, Keith.

I'm deeply indebted to James Coombes, Tim Huckabay, Nicole Cohen and Michelle Eichelberger; my grown-ups. And to Tena Bossert, Anna Huckabay and Edward Bossert; my children. Without their antics, weirdness and eagerness to be outdoors, I'd have had--way too often--no stories to tell.

This is for the memory of Robert Huckabay, the Old Man (my father) and for Ray Fontes, my dad (my stepfather) and to my mother, Dorothy, who made possible my mentoring by each of them. When I needed to be outside, somewhere, they never questioned me; they simply held the door.

Thanks to Bob Hernbrode, who supported my writing more that he will ever know.

Thanks to Morris Uebelacker and Robert Kuhlken and my colleagues at Central Washington University for their encouragement.

Thanks to all those mentioned in these pages...to all the mentors and friends who've invited me to come play at one time or another.

And special thanks to Sam--Carol Samantha Taylor Mazur--for her love and support.

v

THE CONTRIBUTORS

THE AUTHOR

Photo by Debbie Young

James L. Huckabay grew up in the Northwest. After a stint in the U.S. Air Force, he landed in Denver in 1963. Except for a three-year trip to Lawrence, Kansas, for a Ph.D. in Geography and Meteorology, Jim stayed in the Denver, where he taught at the University of Colorado, owned and operated an environmental consulting business and worked for a number of Colorado's wildlife and sportsmen's organizations. During that time, he worked for a number of years as a radio/TV weatherman, had a weekly radio program (*The Rockies Outdoors*) and syndicated a daily three-minute radio program (*Inside the Outdoors*) to 50 stations in nine western states. In 1993, he returned to the Northwest and settled in Kittitas County, in central Washington. He teaches in the Department of Geography and Land Studies at Central Washington University in Ellensburg.

Over the past decade or so, Jim has written hundreds of newspaper columns, and researched and written another 150 or so watchable wildlife features, brochures, publications and training documents. Currently, his book, *Conversations With an Old Mountain Man*, is awaiting a publication decision at a small publishing house in upstate New York.

THE PAINTER

Photo by Ellen Bennett

Parks Reece is a classically-trained artist working in acrylics. He just happens to have a strange way of looking at the world he paints. As writer Tim Cahill has summed up Parks' style: "Here's training and talent shackled to an altogether peculiar perception of our natural world."

Parks Reece grew up in the country around North Wilkesboro, North Carolina, more-or-less under the guidance of his mother Gwyn, a nationally-known painter. After a journey befitting his outdoor interests, he landed in Livingston, Montana.

Parks' popularity has grown rapidly, and his work is currently being used in several publications. A book devoted to his paintings and perspective is in the works.

All the paintings reproduced in this book are available as color laser xerograph prints (and some of the originals may also be available).

For further information about these paintings, or one or another of the recent books featuring Parks' work, contact the Parks Reece Gallery, at

The Murray Hotel
201 West Park Street
Livingston, MT 59047
(406) 222-1350

THE SKETCH ARTISTS

Tena Bossert (top right-- age 14 at the time of publication), Anna Huckabay (left--13) and Edward Bossert (bottom--9) are the last of the author's offspring.

Tena, Anna and Edward have been doing pen and ink drawings, pencil sketches, and using various other media for creating images since they were kids.

They live in the foothills of the Rocky Mountains, a good day's hike southwest of Denver, Colorado.

CONTENTS

Part 1. Living in the Late 20th Century

Part 2. Freebe the WonderDog

Part 3. Wild Winds and Other Adventures

Part 4. Mentors and Friends

Part 5. Spain

Part 6. My Old Man and My Dad

Part 7. Family Marches to Its Own Beat

PREFACE

As you'll gather from reading these stories, I've lived in several parts of the West. I grew up in Wenatchee and Yakima, Washington and Boise, Idaho. After a stint in the U.S. Air Force, I landed in Denver in 1963. Except for a three-year trip to Lawrence, Kansas, for some graduate work, I stayed in the Denver area until 1993, when I responded to an urge to come back to the Northwest and settled here in Kittitas County.

I've been blessed with some great mentors, most of whom you'll meet here. This book is for all of them.

I've also been blessed with an abundance of offspring: I have children and adults. In here, you will see references to my now-adults (James, Tim, Nicole and Michelle), and stories about my children (Tena, Anna and Edward) who've contributed drawings for some of the stories herein. You may also meet a couple of their mothers.

Many of these stories came from playing in the outdoors with friends and family. Others came from years of working in broadcasting and sportsmen's organizations and working both for and against various wildlife and government agencies. Still, they are *all* about people, and those universal questions we ask about our relationships to each other, the earth and other living things.

To help create context, I've included the dates the stories were written. For the most part, these are from my column "Inside The Outdoors," which appeared in the *Douglas County News-Press*, a daily on the south end of the Denver Metro Area, and *The Ellensburg Weekly*, published here in Kittitas County, in Central Washington. The *Weekly*'s offices are on Pearl Street, hence the names you'll see for the very loosely-organized group of citizens making up our local "think tank benevolent association." One or another of our "members" often provided the fodder for a column or two.

As you read these stories, you'll guess that some plans worked out and others never came to fruition. You'd be guessing right.

Funny thing, how life goes...

A Childhood Myth ©1986   Parks Reece

PART ONE

LIVING IN THE LATE 20TH CENTURY

YELLOWSTONE

(HOT SPRINGS & WILD THINGS)

(September, 1995) Funny the things you think about at those way-way-off-Pearl Street meetings of the Pearl Street Working Dog, Free Beer & Outdoor Think Tank Benevolent Association. And how an off-the-cuff remark can change the scenery.

One Saturday earlier this month of September (the 9th, as I recall), we converged on Mammoth Hot Springs, in Yellowstone, to help Robert Kuhlken and Cynthia Acker tie the knot. Bob is a new faculty member in Geography and Land Studies at Central, so it seemed like about the least we could do.

Ken and Jo Hammond drove in from Ellensburg. Samantha and I were playing in Yellowstone on our way back home from Colorado. Other friends and family of the happy couple had rolled in from places like Montana, Oregon, Minnesota and points east. Both place and weather were perfect, and we got them properly witnessed and wed.

After cake and appropriate libations, we drove about halfway to Gardiner, Montana, toward the north entrance to the park. Our wedding party then wandered a half-mile or so up the Gardiner River. After we were seated on the rocks and gravels beneath the high, steep cliffs towering over the river, the PSWDFB&OTTBA meeting was called to order.

Bob worked in Yellowstone for a while once upon a time, and this gathering of new and old friends and family was a symbolic step into his new life with Cynthia... and Central. He was explaining all that to me as we tried to get comfortable on the rocks and gravel next to the Gardiner River. This had always been a favorite place of his.

Several of us were admiring the high cliffs as we listened to the roar of the Gardiner tumbling along a few feet away. Bob turned to me, casually waving at those cliffs. "That's where the bighorn sheep always seemed to hang out.." Right then, something changed. Those giant walls no longer just framed our field meeting of the PSWDFB&OTTBA. Now they became ripe with possibility: bighorns at any moment!

As several pairs of eyes glued themselves to that canyon wall, I started thinking about hunting and watching and being connected with wildlife. And why Sam and I love to play in Yellowstone.

What is it about even the possibility of seeing wild things in wild places that so touches us? That even changes how we see a hillside?

Maybe its some deep thing that hunters have always known. Something that others are seeking to reach now. I often think that wildlife stands as an icon, a symbol, of the state of all our living, growing natural resources. Maybe being touched by some wild thing in some wild, rugged country helps us know that however human society goes, the wild places and we ourselves--and life itself--may yet be okay.

Interactions (and even the expectation of interactions) with wild things stir in us a deep, primal, cellular knowing about our belonging to the earth. Those interactions affect our lives in ways unknown to people who don't feel connected with the earth and her creatures.

Many hunters seem to believe that one must hunt--be among wild things with some intent--to have that earth connection. I've said that, too. But maybe humans do not have to hunt to be fully connected with wildlife and the earth which sustains us all. Look at traditional farming and rural communities, where people don't always hunt, but are, generally, deeply in sync with the life surrounding them.

I often feel that the lost sense of connection with our fellow living things is THE underlying human/wildlife interaction issue of our time. Sure, hunting and fishing are time-proven vehicles for allowing people to find their oneness with nature. Unfortunately, we can no longer fit EVERYONE who wants that connection into the field to fish and hunt. Watchable wildlife opportunities--with the interest and education they engender--can help people make that connection. Anything we can do to help people find their place of "belonging" with wildlife will help ensure the future of our wildlife. That's why places like Yellowstone are so important.

We need an educated public. We need people who understand the wild things well enough to help keep those resources from disappearing. People wandering around Yellowstone and Grand Teton, and all the places here in Washington where we can watch wild things, begin to get that understanding. Not everyone is going to be a wildlife expert, but only an educated public will work wisely for tomorrow's wildlife.

If enough of us aren't committed to abundant and healthy wildlife and habitat, what will become of our species? To be committed to wildlife and habitat, people have to feel connected to the earth. There, beside the Gardiner River, we were getting connected.

About the time these thoughts had worked their way through my mind, it was time to get out and dry off. (Oops, did I forget to mention that those rocks and gravels we were sitting on were neck-deep under the hot water of the Boiling River where it flows into the Gardiner?)

Having no more pressing business at this most scenic of hot springs, we adjourned to the K-Bar in Gardiner. Sam was about to get her long-time wish to have a cold beer in a cowboy bar in Montana.

Two blocks from the K-Bar, a buck antelope browsed along the street. It had been a good day for a wedding...A good day to start a new life.

I N H U M A N E ?

(August, 1995) I guess I've wondered what "inhumane" means ever since I was a kid. Lately, I've been wondering again.

Nancy Hultquist is an occasional addition to off-Pearl Street meetings of the PSWDFB&OTTBA. She and John raise Brittanys, horses and Cain outside Ellensburg a few miles. Over a few months we've talked a bit about a difficult decision she made about one of her old horses--and the view of a couple friends that her ultimate decision was a terribly inhumane way to treat a horse she loved. Her horse club friends seemed to understood the issue, but others just clammed up or freaked out.

Anyhow, she had this old, worn-out horse. He was starting to have trouble getting up at times. The most humane thing to do was put the animal down, but she also didn't want his body just dumped somewhere. She checked into vet costs and disposal, and the possibility of taking the horse to Cavel West, a horsemeat packing plant in Redmond, Oregon.

To make a long story short, she delivered her horse to Cavel West, and was with him when he was put down. She knew that he would be made into meat for the domestic and overseas market, and was paid a fair price for her horse's carcass. When all was said and done, Nancy felt she had kept her commitment to see that his death was humane.

All the uproar got me thinking about Project WILD!, a program to teach school kids about ecology, conservation and wildlife and its habitat. A few years back, I interviewed Cheryl Charles, its national program director, for my syndicated western radio program. She described Project WILD! as "about the importance of wildlife, about the belief that people can make a difference...and take actions that can be a benefit to people and to wildlife and to the environment in the long term".

I had seen the program being used and knew some of its developers. Games and exercises are designed for kids to see the interrelationships of water, food, shelter, predators and natural disasters. Youngsters quickly understand the impacts of habitat destruction and some basic principles of population dynamics.

Project WILD! has probably reached a million children in 40 states and much of Canada, and more in places as far off as India, Australia, Denmark and Sweden. Sponsors and supporters of the program included such diverse groups as the National Wildlife Federation, the American Humane Association, Defenders of Wildlife and Safari Club International.

About the time of the interview, a group in Boulder, Colorado--Speak Out For Animals--was picketing a teacher training workshop. They intended to get the Boulder Valley School District to drop Project WILD! from its curriculum. Other groups were staging similar actions around the country. The gist of their protest was that some of the lessons went so far as to "lead children to accept hunting as humane."

So. What is "humane?"

When I was six years old, one of my family chores was to catch a chicken, chop off its head and present it to my mother for Sunday dinner. The Old Man instructed me in the careful, quick and humane use of a small ax. We ate a lot of chicken.

The first time I actually remember wondering about what was humane was when I heard and watched a horsefly struggling hopelessly against one of the fly strips we hung in the barn. Now, that was inhumane, I thought, but nobody seemed to care.

Over time, I began to get that "humane" was just for animals and big birds. Still, what some of our old mousetraps did to mice who didn't die right away would again raise the question in my mind.

By the time I was 15, I had it figured. I had been schooled by the Old Man and my favorite uncle Ed in the humane dispatching of a duck, a rabbit, a trout, a bullhead, a pig, a steer or a deer. Whether I made meat in the barn-yard or the field, I took great pride in clean kills. Occasionally, I didn't, but I followed up quickly...and as humanely as possible.

During my 16th year--a tough winter in the mid-50s--I saw things I've never forgotten. Deer by the hundreds moved down into the orchards of the Wenatchee Valley, along Washington's Columbia River. "Orchard hunts" thinned the herds of deer, in attempts to prevent years worth of damage to the fruit trees.

As winter wore on, hundreds of deer began starving to death. Our Explorer Troop got involved with helping the Game and Fish drag carcasses to a deep trench for disposal. It was hard work.

But the hardest thing I've ever done was watch those deer die.

We were not allowed to shoot them. We were allowed to watch other kids trying to "ride" those too weak to run. We were allowed to chase off, but not destroy, people's "pets" as they ripped at the bellies and hamstrings of the deer. We were allowed to watch them struggle to stand again after they sagged or fell to the ground.

And we could watch their eyes empty, then drag their skin-and-bones bodies to the trench and throw them in. From that time on, hunting seemed to me like it had to be pretty humane.

So, what is "humane"? I dunno. Maybe it has something to do with helping a life end with respect...maybe even with love.

PRIORITIES

(January, 1995) How do we get into these conversations? It was a hastily-called, non-quorum meeting of the Pearl Street Working Dog, Free Beer & Outdoor Think Tank Benevolent Association (PSWDFB &OTTBA) at Sweet Memories. With talk of summer came questions about how we had created our outdoor priorities.

It was generally agreed that we develop such things in the process of growing up. For me, though, one moment in time sold me on following my heart.

My folks had split up and my brothers and mom and I had just moved from East Wenatchee, Washington, to Yakima. September of 1958--my junior year in high school. Jackie was beautiful, with a stable, loving and outdoor family. Her father, Ron, was a fisherman and hunter with a cabin on Rimrock Lake...and a water-skiing boat he'd let us use anytime.

On school mornings, I'd get to Naches (where I'd decided to attend high school), have breakfast with the family, then walk to school with Jackie. I always felt welcome. I had liked Ron the moment I met him. A funny guy, he was always joking about how my early morning appearances overflowed his cup of life. I loved my time with them. I never thought about what an impact they might have on a kid who had lived to hunt and fish from his first steps outdoors.

I've told and retold this story so many times through the years that I'm honestly not sure how much is original and how much has been pounded out and repainted. The story itself, however, is true...

The 50s were tough. The recession touched us all, and the ones who could find steady work generally held to it gratefully. Ron had grown up in the East. He moved to Washington as a young man and began a very successful career with Pacific Power and Light. His younger brother, Bob, had stayed in the East, becoming a skilled tool and die maker. Like thousands of Americans, Bob got caught in the recession. He had been searching for work for months, and was growing desperate. He and his family were slowly sinking. Ron figured a change of scenery might help his brother, and invited Bob to come look in the Northwest. He came, while his wife and kids stayed behind to do as they could.

Every morning, Bob had his lunch packed and was eager to hit the streets. Each day was going to be THE day he'd find work. He was the most optimistic man I'd ever met. He was a hunter.

One day, after maybe four weeks of Bob's searching, the breakfast table was even more upbeat than normal. Bob was dressed a little differently--like a man going to work. Jackie said, "Uncle Bob found a PERFECT job. The owner loves his work and he's going to start him at a good wage!" Bob talked about sending for his family as soon as possible. He missed his wife and kids terribly and couldn't wait to settle them into a new home in Yakima. And with an honest man's work again after all these months. Such joy!

This was early October.

Within a week, I walked into a very quiet kitchen. Eyes were on plates and food, no one was joking around. I looked at Jackie. Finally, she told me what was going on. "Uncle Bob asked his boss for some time off", she said. Then Bob picked it up. "I only wanted two weeks. And I certainly don't expect to get paid for it. Hell, I told him I *always*--from the time I was a kid--took two weeks to go deer hunting. And this year I can go with my brother for the first time in I don't know how long. I thought we were getting along great... I really love that job. And he's a great guy. He just doesn't understand..." Silence. Then Jackie said, "His boss said he had to show up for work or get fired..."

Bob shook his head as he got up from the table and grabbed his lunchbox. "I dunno," he said, "but it sure seems to me a damn shame that a man has to quit a good job just to go deer hunting!"

Quit he did. After all he and his family had been through. On opening day of deer season, Bob, Ron and assorted pals were in the woods.

While they were gone, Bob's boss called to see if he was really hunting, and asked Jackie's mom to have Bob call him when he got back.

The Monday after THE HUNT, I got to breakfast just as it broke up. (My cousin and I had returned late from our own weekend deer hunt, and I'd been a little slow getting started.) Bob was already gone. The mood seemed awfully upbeat to me. On the way to school, Jackie filled me in. "...And his boss said he just had to know if Uncle Bob was REALLY a man of his word. He not only gave him his job back, but he gave him a little raise--'cause his work is so good--and said he could have his two weeks a year, without pay of course, in addition to his regular paid vacation...and he may give Uncle Bob a chance to buy the company when he retires in a couple years. And my aunt's coming next week...can you believe it? Daddy says its just the way it was supposed to work out. Wow."

That fall Monday morning I understood about following one's heart... about priorities for time with nature and time with good work. And maybe a little something about integrity, too.

As our little PSWDFB&OTTBA broke up, someone asked about Ron and Jackie. Some years ago, I wrote Ron, thanking him for taking me in the way he did. Last year, I found out he's catching big kokanees in some clear, cold lake on life's other side. Jackie and her family are in the lower Yakima valley.

K
O
K
A
N
E
E
SNAGGING

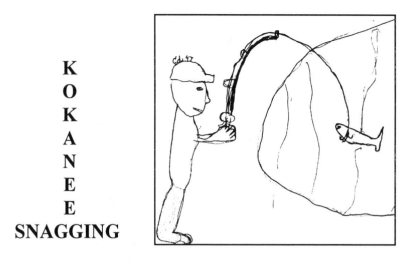

(AND SO-CALLED "SPORTSMANSHIP")

(November, 1988) Ever do any kokanee snagging?   It ain't your plain run-of-the-mill fishing. And there seems to be plenty of folks around these days to tell us it ain't sportsmanlike, either.

So What?

It isn't fishing. And it isn't sportsmanlike. And It IS food-gathering. There are rules and skills involved, but it is no more a "sport" than picking wild chokecherries.

Still, as I look around Colorado's fishing and outdoor community, I see no shortage of people trying to eliminate snagging; trying to define snagging as a "sport" so that they can then deal with it from a perspective of "ethical" and "sporting". Strikes me that they've lost their ability to hold a perspective.

Back during my high school years, in eastern Washington, I fished for kokanees. We trolled hardware and we caught them on bait. This was in the spring and summer between my junior and senior years of high school. I had been going with Jackie Nelson most of that junior year, and her dad, Ron, took a shine to me.   In the late spring and summer, Ron taught me his kokanee secrets up on Rimrock Lake. Oh man! Catching those feisty little kokes was exciting. THAT was real fishing! After the boat was safely put away, Ron would smoke some of those succulent ten- to thirteen-inch salmon over chunks of green aspen limbs. To this day, I've never eaten anything better. I loved their rich, pink flesh broiled, baked or fried.

My first experience with snagging the little landlocked salmon came a few years later, in the mid 1960s. It wasn't long after I landed at Lowry Air Force Base. One of the civilian employees was talking about the fall kokanee runs, and offered to take me along on a "food-gathering" expedition to Granby and the Shadow Mountain Reservoir spillway.

The salmon die after spawning in their third or fourth year, so the Division of Wildlife allows generous limits of the fish for those who wish to snag them in certain restricted areas. Since their eggs rarely survive the winters in Colorado, the wildlife guys collect the eggs and milt, hatch the fish in a controlled environment, then release them each year in various reservoirs and feeder streams around the state. During the three or four years that follow, the salmon will reach ten to twenty inches in length. Until nature draws them back to the release site to spawn, the fish will provide great "sport" fishing.

At any rate, this fellow lived with his elderly mother, and the salmon he collected during these expeditions provided them with many high-quality meals during the year. This man was not a hunter--he just couldn't bring himself to personally kill an animal--although he enjoyed beef and pork, and the game meat friends gave him. Since the fish would die once they had spawned, anyway, he simply looked upon the harvest as a gift of food from God and the fish themselves. He was a grateful man.

I joined him on a cold November Saturday. In places, the stream below the spillway was literally red with salmon fourteen to sixteen inches in length, and up to almost two pounds. In a matter of three or four hours we had snagged our limits. I had even reached into the water and grabbed some kokes with my gloved hand. The 30 or so pounds of firm, pink salmon I had to show for the day were a blessing.

Over the years, I have snagged for salmon along Carter Reservoir, Green Mountain, Dillon, Cheesman, and others, as well as a few streams. The fish have ranged greatly in size, from ten inches to eighteen inches, and up to nearly three pounds. The weather during these trips has been everything from sunny and warm to icy, windy and colder than you- know-what.

Snagging has always been an adventure, and it's always fun to meet fellow snaggers and watch their families. Snaggers, with their heavy rods, weighted treble hooks and special buckets, take their food-gathering seriously. The best snaggers have certain skills, or "senses"--they just know where and how to work the grounds. Being with snaggers is a lot like meeting people out picking wild berries or chokecherries, or running into folks looking for the first wild asparagus or mushrooms of spring.

A year ago, I figured a family outing for salmon-snagging up at Cheesman Reservoir would provide us a little exercise and a good excuse for a picnic. Maybe even supplement our winter meat supply. Rumor had it that the kokanee spawning in the Goose Creek inlet were big and firm, and hitting a peak in numbers. It would be just a pleasant hike across the dam, so off we went with Tena and Anna (our two pre-schoolers) in tow.

We soon discovered that the Denver Water Board had closed the road across the dam to pedestrians. The walk around was arduous: way, way down to the river and way, way back up. At least a couple miles more than we were willing to carry, or drag, the girls. We learned from a family of successful snaggers that they had walked across the dam before dawn, but found it closed on their way out. Carrying their heavy harvest of salmon back to the parking area had turned into an afternoon's tough work. Still, they spoke joyfully of the "gift" of these salmon.

The Division of Wildlife has begun curtailing places and times when snagging can take place. Fisheries biologists have expressed the intention of doing away with salmon snagging as soon as enough support can be found. This is taking place in response to the whining of some biologists and "sport" fishermen about "sportsmanship." Bull.

Maybe I'll go salmon snagging again. And maybe not. Whatever, I will continue to appreciate the gift of the salmon. And I will more and more resent the judgements and ill-informed statements of so-called "purists" who see salmon-snagging as some sleazy activity performed by people with no understanding of sportsmanship.

IS salmon snagging "sporting"? Hell, no! And so what? Picking wild chokecherries, gathering firewood, picking up fallen apples and snagging salmon are HARVESTING activities. These harvests help sustain us, physically and spiritually. Tucked inside them is a joy and gratitude for the gifts of Mother Earth and our wild brothers and sisters. We must be grateful and responsible for these gifts, but that has little to do with some phony idea of "sportsmanship".

EARTH BISCUITS

(August, 1995) Like most everybody else lately, I've been putting up for the winter. There's that thing that touches us when we make fruit or vegetables or meat for the cold season ahead...some way-down-deep thing that reminds us who we are and how our well-being is directly related to how we cultivate and live with the Earth. There's something about looking at jars of canned cherries and peaches that's more satisfying than TV. Like you're making a promise to be here and be well through winter. Or something. Makes me think about "earth biscuits".

Cousin Ron and I were talking about a trip to Wyoming to make antelope meat. And elk hunting here. We were sitting at his place in Terrace Heights in Yakima during last week's cool fall-like weather. You know how that feels... About this time every year: even when the sun's out, you can feel that crispness in the air. There's an edge to it so sharp that it slices almost painlessly to that place where the deer and elk and antelope live...that place where we belong to the natural land. Anyhow, Ron was suggesting I get a muzzleloader and go after a fat cow elk. He reminded me how we always enjoyed preparing and freezing a cow as much any bull we ever crossed destinies with.

Ron got me thinking of the first time I heard about "earth biscuits"...

Brad looked at me in that exasperated way that almost-men look at middle-aged men who don't get it. He was assessing the woman who more or less coordinated the community of people around Villa Grove, in the San Luis Valley in Colorado. "Earth biscuit," he said. "C'mon. Live off the land, wholesome, made-from-scratch, committed to earth, hot springs, all natural...You know--an earth biscuit!". I got it.

We were in the valley to make antelope and deer meat--me with my bow and Brad with a muzzleloader. Brad's father Roy, an old friend of mine, owned a piece of the ranch we were hunting. Our conversation had centered around those I had known as hippies--those of the 60s who dropped out of mainstream society to find or re-establish their earth roots. We talked of the people of the 80s who were looking at their place with earth. Bradley, on the other hand, was more concerned about college, and why rain caused his muzzleloader to misfire. "Not hippies," he muttered, with a glint in his eye, "in the 80s it's earth biscuits!"

When my grown-ups were still teenagers, we lived in Denver. Most of our back yard was devoted to a garden which helped us meet a fair part of our food needs. Our closest neighbors had wall to wall grass, a sprinkler system which ran even in the rain and a most decidedly negative transplanted-New-York attitude about our hunting.

Al and Sue were particularly disgusted about our habit of hanging fresh antelope, deer or elk carcasses in the back yard for a few hours while we washed them down and allowed them to air dry, We would then move them to a cool out-of-sight place until we processed the meat. One Sunday afternoon, when I was cleaning an antelope carcass, Al demanded to know why I had to insult him and his wife with the bodies of these poor dead creatures. I was at a loss for words, since these guys loved fine steaks and meat of all kinds. Finally, I simply explained to him what I was doing, so that when we cut the meat, it would be free of dirt and hair and leaves, and so on. This was important, I said, since this animal had given us meat which would help sustain our family through the coming year. After a short pause, he looked at the carcass. "So where do the steaks come from?"

When they came over we had parts all over the kitchen. They watched as the meat became sausage, burger, steaks and the rest. Little was said. A few weeks later, at a party, I overheard Sue talking with friends. "...And we used to really get upset, but you know what? They use every scrap--they even make their own sausage. We learned about why some meat's more tender than other meat. And its really good meat!"

A couple years after all that, I got a call from a woman named Beth. Beth was involved in a "mastery" training program run by my friends Stephen Buhner and Trishuwa. During that training, Beth had come to feel that she was supposed to help others learn to live in a whole way, to honor Earth's gifts of life, and to explore the responsible taking, and use, of those gifts. First, however, she had to know it personally. She had heard that, in our hunting, we asked for permission to take the life of an animal before taking it. And that we honored that gift when it was given. She had reservations about hunting, but understood that all food--seed, vegetable or meat--was produced by something alive. Would I be willing to help her understand the choices and responsibilities and joy involved in making meat?

Beth took her Hunter Safety Course, as I requested, and joined me for a deer hunt the last evening of the season. We didn't see the buck I was sure was nearby, but such times are magic anyway. As darkness and a light rain spread over the foothills north of Denver, that hunter's sense of belonging to the Earth settled over us.

A month later, two of my grownups (they're hardly kids anymore) and I took three deer on a special late-season hunt. Beth came over to help with the meat processing. She was into it from cleaning carcass pieces to grinding fat trimmings for the ravens and magpies. Late in the afternoon, she looked up from trimming stew pieces and said, in her best earth biscuit voice, "I got it. The joy here is what you feel when you're putting up food from your garden...food you're responsible for." She eventually understood the rest of it, too, from that Earth-connected place inside. Earth biscuits are like that.

Garlic Eaters Live Longer
©1996 Parks Reece

MEMORY-BANK SAVINGS ACCOUNTS

(January, 1996) The concept is very simple. You put something into the bank.

I've long thought that a big part of the value of a fishing or hunting trip is that we "bank" the enjoyment, and can relive the experience.

Of course, not everyone understands the concept. After I finished my graduate work, I labored for a summer on a grounds crew at Lowry Air Force Base in Denver.

One of the other crew members was a fisherman and hunter who'd "spent a month too long in Vietnam," as he put it. Dave came home, bought an old school bus, painted it in psychedelic colors and designs, and started making and selling silver and bead jewelry. (He said he added the "Jesus Saves" stickers when he found that southern cops would shake their heads, but only smile and wave when they passed him. He said it kept his drug stash safe.) Anyway, we were talking about reliving trips over lunch one day. "That's what I like most about doing acid," he said. "You pay for one trip and you get all kinds of repeats free--sometimes months later!" Dave was around through fall that year. He wanted me to introduce him to Colorado's hunting, but, as I recall, I just got too busy.

The concept was best explained by a writer for one of the outdoor mags sometime in the middle 60s. I didn't hang onto the column, but I held dearly to the man's argument. He wrote of opening a "memory-bank" account. Into this account would go all of your memories of outdoor trips and activities--hunting, fishing, camping, hikes with your kids and par-ents, and so forth. The beauty of this kind of account is that you make withdrawals as often as you like but the account never gets drawn down. In fact, every time you take a favorite memory out of your "memory- bank", you polish it, treasure it, enjoy it, and by the time you use it and return it, it's worth more than when you withdrew it from the account. I figure THAT'S how a trip ought to be relived!

To this day, I can almost see the last paragraph in that writer's column. I'm making these lines up, but they were something like: "So remember this. Nothing is more important than making regular deposits into your account. When you're 80 or 90 years old, which will serve you best? The polished and carefully-saved memories of times afield with buddies and those you love? Or the memories of the papers which crossed your desk, or the widgets which passed on the line before you? So, do your work with pride...but make those "memory-bank" deposits."

One of the things I like about this is that when I get serious about keeping the account growing, the Universe throws in a bonus. Just before Christmas, I kept my promise to take Sam salmon fishing, but I didn't tell her and sixteen-year-old daughter Stacey where we were going. After only minor grumbling about the hour, we found ourselves unloading gear at the gate for Sport Fishing of Seattle on Pier 54. It was 6:15 AM.

By 6:40 we'd met Captain Jim Moore and Deck-hand Shari Stoican, and were on our way into what would have been a beautiful day even in October. We'd be fishing for immature chinook salmon (blackmouths, they're called) and cohos.

We were not 45 minutes into our day before we were surrounded by orcas. (We've been out on the Sound before, looking for orcas and enjoying wildlife, but we'd never got the orcas part.) We were close enough to identify the big male of the pod, the females and a calf. In an instant, sleepiness was gone, and that bonus in the bank.

Salmon began hitting fairly quickly, and I landed the first keeper blackmouth (about six pounds). Not long later, Sam caught a beautiful little coho. Soon after, as Stacey was ready to give up fishing for a bit, I hooked a very nice blackmouth and handed the rod to Sam, intending for her to land the fish. She handed it off to Stacey and we all waved good-bye to the nice salmon. After an hour or so of catching flounder and sole (and a few small salmon), Stacey hooked the biggest blackmouth of the day. The closer it got to the boat, the more she knew she couldn't land it. But she did. A beautiful salmon and seven pounds worth of exhausted smiles! The rest of the day was a blur of seals, waterfowl, eagles, sole, flounder and squid (somehow, Shari found time to cook up some calamari right there on the boat!)--and a bit more salmon action. Did I mention how beautiful it was out there?

We brought back our three salmon and filets of several decent flounder and sole. I love this: we get our fish and our pictures, and we all still have stuff left over for massive deposits into our individual accounts.

The late L.L. Bean, the guy who started the mail-order sporting goods business, had it figured out. He took his business very seriously (he was the first to offer his customers their money back if they were dissatisfied *for any reason*). Every employee had to be an outdoor nut of some ilk, and every item sold by the company was (still is) field tested by the employees. The man was also serious about his play time. When he was in his 80s, he was still going strong, fishing and hunting at every opportunity. He noticed one day that he was on the stream with several of the same men he'd fished and hunted with as a boy. They were all reaching old age blessed with good health. "It dawned on me," he said, "that the Good Lord must not count against the sum of a man's days, those days spent in pursuit of fish and game."

(And maybe, just maybe, He won't count those hours I spend counting the treasure in my memory-bank account.)

Anyhow, at worst, we all added a day to our lives out there. Hell, Jim Moore and Shari Stoican may live forever.

THE WATERTON CANYON BIGHORN SHEEP DIE-OFF

(October, 1988) I didn't get it.

That was certainly obvious to the biologist sitting across the conference table that afternoon. "But you don't understand," he said. "We're going to have the best documented die-off in the history of bighorn sheep management in North America!"

The subject of the meeting was construction of the Strontia Springs Dam--on the South Platte River just southwest of metro Denver--and its effect on the herd of 80 to 120 bighorns that lived above and along the river in Waterton Canyon. At the time of the meeting, truck traffic was heavy in the canyon. Construction was underway--and so was the die-off.

I was president of the Rocky Mountain Bighorn Society at the time, and to say that we were concerned about our worst fears coming true would be an understatement. Studies and observations elsewhere had shown that sheep under stress were highly susceptible to pneumonia and lungworm. The sheep in this canyon were confined to it by dense stands of oakbrush. Since bighorns rely so heavily on their eyes for protection, these sheep steered clear of the brush. They would, thus, be unable to simply walk away from the dust, noise and traffic. We had many times expressed the concern that, given the poor, closed-in habitat, the added stress would simply kill off the sheep.

Through many generations, the Waterton Canyon sheep had formed a unique, low-elevation herd. In a very real sense, these sheep represented a unique "gene pool" worthy of preservation. The Society's position was that there ought to be a way to keep the herd viable.

As it became apparent that the dam *would* be built, we met with the various powers-that-be in attempts to negotiate, or cause to be negotiated, a positive treatment of the bighorn sheep. DOW, the Division of Wild- life was responsible for the wildlife in the canyon. Since 1944, DOW biologists had trapped and transplanted over 1,000 bighorns from the canyon to various new homes in Colorado and elsewhere around the West. There were sites to which the Waterton Canyon bighorns could be moved (at least enough of them to create a viable herd). They could then be returned to the canyon after construction.

This "moving and returning" was suggested a number of times, but rejected by the DOW biologists for a variety of reasons. A great deal of work needed to be done in the canyon to ensure that the bighorns would have an open, healthful habitat which would support a strong herd. If the sheep were removed, the Water Department could possibly renege on its commitment to protect the sheep and improve the habitat in the canyon. Removing a portion of the herd to a safe temporary habitat could create the same problem. Besides, with all the biologists monitoring the sheep, what could possibly go wrong?

Plenty. By the time of the meeting I mentioned above, more than a dozen sheep were dead and at least that many more were walking around on wobbly legs, or having obvious difficulty breathing. By then it was far too late to consider moving the sheep. Better to keep a close eye on them and see if some key could be found to prevent such a die-off in the future.

Some of the sick sheep were shot by biologists so that the necropsies, or whatever, could be performed at various stages of the illnesses. Hundreds of photos of diseased lungs and sick and dead sheep were taken. We were treated to scientific discussions of the diseases, the habitat problems, and the roles of stress and dust in the die-off. We talked about how the sheep would stand calmly watching the construction traffic, breathing the dust, and yet die of stress within days because the closed-in habitat left them no way out of the canyon. When Dr. Joe Zbylski suggested treatment with various antibiotics, DOW responses centered on impracticality, cost, how such treatments were unproven on sheep, and how most of the bighorns would probably live anyway.

When it was over, and the construction crews pulled out, there were-- maybe--fifteen sheep in Waterton Canyon. In spring of 1984, after lambing, there were seventeen or eighteen. Habitat work has since been done in the canyon, with hand clearing and burning of oakbrush and fertilizing and planting of favored grasses of the sheep. Much of this work has been done by the Water Board, and much by neighboring Martin-Marietta, the Bighorn Society, the Forest Service and other interested parties. All to make the canyon a viable home for a healthy, unique, herd of sheep.

Today, the canyon supports 15 bighorns. The biologist who oversaw the sheep die-off is now a regional biologist for the DOW. Several graduate students wrote great, vivid, papers and graduated. Other sheep, in other places, are still dying and being researched to death. But we have one helluva well documented die-off.

And I STILL don't get it.

COMP-U-DUCK

(September, 1995) It was one of those end-of-August afternoons. You know: sunny and pleasant, with just enough edge to put you in mind of a crisp fall morning in a duck blind. I could almost see a brace of fat northern mallards checking my decoys when Roger Reynolds picked up his phone. I'd called to fill him in on his responsibilities as the Vantage Field Rep to the Pearl Street Working Dog, Free Beer & Outdoor Think Tank Benevolent Association--and to see if he could come play.

When he's not guiding duck hunters out in the Columbia Basin, Roger professes in the Communication Department hear at Central. Priorities being what they are in late August, we talked about waterfowl.

Turned out he'd recently been to a Wildlife Commission meeting--the meeting about waterfowl seasons and regulations. We talked about the state biologists and the U.S. Fish and Wildlife Service (F&WS), and how their regulatory work is starting to resemble that of someone who's taken on the job of keeping a pendulum from swinging side to side without stopping the clock...or something like that. And about Alaskan earth-quakes and bears and dusky Canada geese and disgusted Oregon water-fowlers and farmers (trust me, they're related..but that's another story), and mostly about complicated rules and regulations.

That last one resurrected a seven-year-old plan to help my fellow waterfowlers stay within the rules, while making my fortune. Like all of my really great ideas, that brainstorm started innocently enough.

Once upon a time in Colorado, I did a Saturday morning outdoor radio talk show. One of my guests was Dick Hopper. Dick, a biologist with the Colorado Division of Wildlife, was in the thick of the division's battle with the U.S. F&WS. This particular battle was over the cuts the feds had proposed for the 1988-89 duck seasons. State biologists felt that the duck numbers and habitat conditions did not warrant the severe restrictions the feds wanted. It was obvious to the state guys (who considered the feds' data the rough equivalent of what geese leave on golf greens), that duck hunting was about to be even more complicated.

Today, it's still pretty complicated. Our split season is gone this year, replaced with a nice long season from noon on October 14 through next January 21. And the daily limit has gone up a notch to six ducks: not more than five mallards (only one may be a hen), not more than two pintails (of either sex), not more than two redheads, and not more than one canvasback. The possession (in the freezer) limit's complex, too, but the season hasn't started yet, so we'll deal with that later.

Remember that shooting hours change every week. And don't forget that being discovered carrying shells with lead shot--even by oversight--will cost you money and pride. Check your shells with a magnet before leaving home. This year, bismuth shot is legal, too (it's as heavy as lead, but a billion times more expensive), so find a bismuth detector.

So, how'll I serve the overburdened waterfowler and make my bundle?

Say hello to "COMP-U-DUCK"...the first fully portable computerized sensor system designed to aid and protect the honest duck hunter.

COMP-U-DUCK will automatically scan your equipment before you leave home to ensure that your shotshells are legal, you've brought the right decoys and camo, and that you've brought lunch and approved drinks. Its built-in GPS system will locate the zone in which you are hunting, and it will flash a camo-colored light (to avoid alerting the birds which may be coming in to your decoys) at the precise moment you may begin shooting. Trouble identifying species or sex? On its color monitor, COMP-U-DUCK will identify all ducks flying within one mile of your blind. Further, it will show you how these birds will look from various angles, at differing speeds, at distances from 10 to 60 yards and under changing sky conditions. Naturally, one of the main features of this remarkable "hunter's companion" is its ability to keep track of the birds you've bagged. As your hunt continues, it will update you on which ducks remain legal for you and up to three companions--both for your daily limits and your possession limits.

Your self-contained COMP-U-DUCK will weigh less than a small duf-fel bag of decoys. This weatherproof unit will operate for the entire season on two AA batteries. An optional coffee maker will make your time in the blind more pleasant, as will the automatic heater. Built-in scanners will grunt if you are being watched by an agent with binoculars or spotting scope. At the precise end of legal shooting hours, your COMP-U-DUCK will emit a crude, but all-natural, noise.

We are busily working up the programming as I write this, and expect to have COMP-U-DUCK available shortly. It will not be cheap, but not out of line with the cost of chronometers, state and federal duck stamps, F&WS salaries, decoys, shells, leases, blinds, habitat and good dogs. (Part of our challenge is to keep our program from being confused with COOK-U-GOOS, the program apparently used by F&WS.)

I need the money: order yours now, and one for a friend.

Oh, yes. If you've had no action for one hour, COMP-U-DUCK will challenge you to answer questions like this: What happens to duck hunt-ing--and the bureaucrats who run it--when those of us who buy licenses, stamps and equipment, and put up our spare change (and then some) for waterfowl habitat, decide that it is no longer worth all the harassment?

Opening Day Surprise
©1987 Parks Reece

The Late 20th Century   26

PART TWO

FREEBE
THE WONDER DOG

THE COMING OF FREEBE

(March, 1995) The topic on the floor was the name change. Several regulars were of the opinion that "Pearl Street Columnist, Gadfly & Think Tank Benevolent Association" (PSCG&TTBA) was too restrictive a handle: our name had to reflect more of our broad-based interests as outdoor citizens of the county--even if we kept our headquarters on Ellensburg's Pearl Street.

"So, what ARE our interests, anyhow?" Chris finally asked. "We *have* taken a stand for free lunches and beer," came a voice from next to the stove. "And dogs. We like working dogs. Like that one that owned Huckabay's 'heirloom' shotgun... that 'Freebe the Wonder Dog'..."

We were quickly out of order and into dog stories. Eventually, some kind soul offered something for my thirst, and I agreed to introduce the Think Tank to Freebe. I wanted to hear the story again, myself, anyway.

In summer of 1970, we moved to Lawrence, Kansas. I was determined to finish my graduate work, and to relax and recreate outdoors even though I was broke. Buddy Rick (in Colorado) had instilled in me the joy of hunting, fishing and playing with a good dog. I wanted one.

Becky, my wife of the time, had the idea that we couldn't afford to feed a dog--even if it ate dirt. Knowing that she would be unable to resist the charms of a puppy, and figuring that the kids didn't need to eat so much now that the school fed them lunch, I joined the Topeka Retriever Club (TRC). It seemed the logical place to start. I figured it might help me find a dog on terms I could afford--like nothing down and nothing a month.

A bit before Thanksgiving, the club received a little lab puppy from good hunting and show lines. There would be a raffle. Five bucks a ticket, as I recall. With some deception and a little creative bookkeeping, I got one raffle ticket. Sometimes you just feel lucky.

The raffle was set for about a week after the holiday. I missed the drawing, but waited for the call. (I REALLY believed that pup was mine!) Becky seemed to be praying, too. After a few days, I was ready to call the president. He beat me to it. Congratulations were in order, he said, the original winner's lab had just whelped a big litter, and he had no room for the pup. Then they drew my name.

Before he hung up, I was out the door and rolling toward his house in Topeka. Becky did not look like a woman whose prayers had been answered.

I was impressed with how genuinely pleased he was to see me get the pup. "What name?" He asked. "Freebe," I said, "TRC's Freebe Jay!"

Freebe won every heart in the family within minutes--as if we had all been together forever. In time, he became a great hunter and the best friend and finest teacher I ever had. He had a great sense of humor. To this day, I know I would not have made it through graduate school without him. Many times, I marveled at the perfection of that dog.

After he had won his third or fourth puppy stakes in the TRC Fun Trial Series, I found out how I REALLY got him. It seems the first winner's dog had, indeed, whelped a big litter, but the winner thought the pup too ugly. The second winner's wife had threatened divorce if she had to feed one more dog. The third winner, as I recall, was moving and didn't want any more dogs. As the beleaguered officers prepared to draw yet another name during a hastily called meeting, someone yelled "No! To hell with it, I know Huckabay will take it. Draw his name.."

Freebe became a very large lab--110 lean pounds. His eyes were deep and intelligent, like few four-legged (or two-legged, for that matter) ani-mals I ever knew.

Too few years later, even the vets at Colorado State University didn't have an answer, but figured that the hip problems had to do with his size. For some reason, the nerves in his hind quarters were dead. After two surgeries, he was literally dragging his atrophied back end, walking entirely on his front legs. Sometimes he seemed in pain, but mostly just bewildered. One day, I held him as the vet squeezed the syringe, and I felt his soul leave his body. I cried for us, and for the deep emptiness inside me.

A few years later, I came across a special photo. In the picture with me were former brother-in-law Claude, and Freebe the Wonder Dog. Freebe was sitting between us, having just delivered a rooster pheasant. He had that look he always had when he'd retrieved a bird in tough cover. It was taken on the Rocky Mountain Arsenal, circa 1975.

Not so long after finding that photo, I stumbled across a possible explanation. Maybe. By that time, the Arsenal had become an EPA Superfund Cleanup Site. It had been declared one of the most polluted areas in North America, after decades of chemical weapon (nerve gas?) and pesticide manufacturing and dumping. The U.S. Army was spending a pile of our tax dollars on the cleanup.

That "possible explanation" showed up as I was half paying attention to a pile of newspaper clippings on my desk, on one of those mornings when the air had that crisp fall feel and taste. If I couldn't be afield, I would waste my time thinking about what was going on out there. Mostly, I was just drifting, when that story drifted to the top of the pile.

According to the article, the Denver Museum of Natural History was about to spend $450,000 of the Army's money. They wanted to find out how the wildlife on the Rocky Mountain Arsenal was faring during the big cleanup which was finally underway. Actually, they were going to work with the small animals and songbirds and raptors which inhabit those areas being disturbed by cleanup on the Arsenal's 27 sections of land.

I can vouch that those 27 square miles support an amazing variety of wildlife. I'd spent a lot of time there. And not by myself.

Anyhow, the museum's personnel would receive medical examinations and special training before they began their fieldwork in spring of 1991. The scientists would also be wearing special protective gear, and would be working only around those sites which were "less contaminated," whatever that meant.

To me, this was fascinating. And scary. And pretty sad.

Remember that photo I'd found?

Claude and I were members of the Arsenal's Rod and Gun Club. We hunted doves, ducks and pheasants there, and fished a bit.

We shot a lot of pheasants over those few years, and we ate every one of them. We never thought much about eating the birds that had been living on the Arsenal, although we were cautioned about not eating the skin and fat of the birds, since any toxins which "may move through the food chain" would be stored there.

We even joked about wanting to hunt the pheasants at night, 'cause we would be able to see them glowing.

As that article started sinking in, I kept remembering something. Freebe retrieved every bird we shot on the Arsenal.

Freebe went down because of the failure of his back legs. When he began suffering, our vets insisted it had to be hip dysplasia, because he was such a big lab.

After the first hip surgery (at about a thousand bucks), however, his hips didn't improve. He was worse, and in more pain. Then I took him to the veterinary school at Colorado State University in Fort Collins. After a five-hundred dollar week of every test they could run, they gave it up. He had NO major nerve impulses to the muscles of his back legs, and that's why they were atrophied. And why he was in such pain.

More and more, Freebe walked only on his front legs. His back legs just dragged behind. It was heart-wrenching. Not long before I made the decision to put him down, he painfully crawled up to me, and laid his head on my lap. I was cleaning "our" shotgun, and he whined, like he was wanting pheasants in his nose again.

As that article became blurry, I kept thinking about all those game birds we took from that pesticide-filled and nerve gas-saturated Arsenal. Who knew? And every one of those birds had been in Freebe's mouth.

For a moment, I wondered if they would like to study me and Claude? Our "protective clothing" was shirts, blue jeans, boots and hunting coats. They could study us real cheap.

Ahh, who cares. It's too late, anyhow, for the best friend I ever had.

I've had other dogs, but I suffer from what my dog buddies called bad luck: a great dog early in my life. Still, I think about ducks and pheasants and quail and geese and four-legged friends. Maybe its time, again.

That story told, it was moved and seconded that the PSCG&TTBA be tentatively known as the Pearl Street Working Dog, Free Beer & Outdoor Think Tank Benevolent Association (PSWDFB&OTTBA), pending further public input.

THE
ROAD
TO
WONDERDOGDOM

(February, 1996) The voice-mail message said something like, "Hi Jim! This is Patrick Hattler. We talked at the American Kennel Club's booth at the International Sportsman's Exposition about finding the pedigree from the '70s for your lab, TRC's Freebe Jay. I wondered if you had any additional information, because we've not been able to find the info you wanted yet. After hearing the story about your lab, we've turned this into a mission. Please get back to me." And he left his number.

Funny thing about working dogs--and labs. At the Expo, Samantha wanted to watch the hunting dogs. We worked our way through the crowds until we were at the fence. The trainers had done a great job with their dogs, and even the pups were quickly and enthusiastically making their retrieves. Sam was enthralled...she kept talking about wanting a pup.

After the demos, and obligatory puppy petting, we wandered over to the American Kennel Club's booth. There I met Patrick Hattler. Somewhere back down the road, I lost Freebe's papers. I keep wanting them back.

Standing there watching those labs going through their paces--living the lives they've been bred to live--really made me yearn for the joy Freebe and I had for a few years. Training him had been a real trip.

"Listen," I remember Maggie saying, "don't overdo his training. This is a really enthusiastic little guy. And smart. Just don't get so wrapped up in 'training' him that you forget God sent him to be your buddy." Maggie was a successful, and terrific, retriever trainer.

This "enthusiastic little guy" was Freebe, a few-months-old black lab puppy already bigger than any other pup the same age. He became the best friend I ever had.

Freebe had come to us through a fund-raising raffle held by the Topeka Retriever Club. I say "to 'us'" because during the early phases of his housetraining and acclimation it seemed important that the family see him as "our" dog. I joined the retriever club in hopes of finding a way to get a good dog, and, after some reluctant winners declined, Freebe came to be "ours". The truth was, I figure, that he and I were meant to be together, but he still loved the rest of the family.

It was nearly spring of 1971. I was determined that the officers and members of the club see that I took winning the dog seriously. It would not do to have Freebe look ill-prepared in the puppy stakes of the spring fun-trial series. Knowing that we had little spare cash on our University of Kansas graduate student budget, Maggie and other club members had really gone out of their way to see that I had training dummies, whistles, pistol blanks, and enough coaching to get Freebe started on his life as a responsible, skilled retriever. Over and over, the trainers cautioned me to not push the pup too much.

I confess I may have been too anxious to get Freebe trained, wanting him at my side in the blind or in pheasant and quail cover. Freebe, however, kept things in balance. He was quick and liked the training, but enough was enough. If I was too serious, or pushed him beyond his enthusiasm, he would take matters into his own paws. He'd walk off a few yards and lay down, yawning his boredom. After a bit, he might come running and growling at me, wanting to wrestle. The pup was a real character, always able to get me to lighten up. Freebe had the tools to be a great hunter--the nose, eyes and desire--but somehow he knew what our partnership would need for success. I began to see that his biggest challenge was to get me trained. It was a tough job.

The puppy stakes at the spring retriever fun trials were not all that difficult. The young dogs just had to perform a couple retrieves. The first was to "sight" retrieve a bird from fairly open cover, and the second setup involved a retrieve from open water. While the handler could have a hand in the pup's collar to keep him steady, the judges still expected to see a pup that would heel, sit and "mark" the fall of the dead pigeon or dummy. We had worked on all aspects of a young retriever's game, and I had seen Freebe's ability. But could he do it with a crowd standing around? What if he refused to go after the bird? What if he ran back to the car and tried to get into his kennel? What if he wouldn't go into the water? What if I forgot what I was supposed to do? What if he didn't do well in all that mud?

This retriever "fun" trial stuff was getting way too serious. We walked away from the crowd. And wrestled. When they called us to the line, Freebe was fine. But he kept checking on me. I was a wreck.

As we walked to the line, my buddies were making comments like "Hey, are you sure that big mutt is only a puppy?" or "Hey, judge, check that dog's papers!" The judges smiled and gave me the instructions and setup: "Now, the blank will be fired there and the dead pigeon will drop over there. We're looking for enthusiasm, attention, nose and clean retrieves. Any questions? OK.. Signal when you're ready."

We were in a vacuum. Dead silence. The gallery was intent on this Topeka Retriever Club raffle pup--and the guy he was training. I looped a short rope through his collar, to steady him. "Ready?" I nodded. "Boom!" The bird was in the air. Freebe watched with an intensity I'd never felt in him before. At the subtle move of my shaky left hand along

his face, pointing toward the bird as it hit the cover, and my sharp "back!" Freebe tore through the mud and into his life.

He delivered the bird to my hand, and re-turned to heel. Applause. As he sat down at my side, he nudged my leg. One of the judges said "Good retrieve. Great enthusiasm!" as he wiped mud splatters off his face.

THE DOG OF CHRISTMAS

(December, 1996) It must be Christmastime. Lately, Freebe the Wonder Dog has been romping in my mind. Freebe owned me for a too-short time. I thought I was teaching him to be a great retriever, but he was actually teaching me about giving and getting love.

I "won" Freebe in a raffle held by a retriever club I had joined. Actually, the officers "drew" my name after the first few winners experienced various kinds of threat and abuse from their spouses. The club officers knew this poor graduate student wanted the pup. My wife was adamant about not keeping the dog--until the moment she met him.

26 years ago this week, we celebrated our first Christmas with that little black bundle of love and energy. 19 years ago, we celebrated without him.

I remember Freebe most at this time of year. Our relationship was a gift of this season. The holiday from classes and teaching really became special. We spent every moment together during this time. Often, in my mind, I return to experience one or another of those times.

Phil Jackson and I took him on his first duck hunt. We were beside a long slough on a lake in eastern Kansas. Things were slow, but late in the morning, Phil knocked down a mallard. The duck landed on the water, along the far bank. Freebe, true to his summer of training and his natural enthusiasm, tore from the blind on command and sailed out into the water.

Unfortunately, the duck was only winged and became evasive. Every time Freebe got close, it dove and disappeared. Now, this is not the experience you want for a young retriever. A dog's enthusiasm and determination to GET THAT BIRD BACK can get him in trouble. After 10 or 15 minutes of swimming in circles, Freebe was exhausted but refusing to come to the whistle without the bird. At last the mallard dove and stayed under.

Somehow, we managed to coax Freebe out of the slough. Phil and I reluctantly decided to forget the duck and go hunt pheasants and quail.

Several hours and birds later, we found ourselves a couple hundred yards from the other side of the slough. Freebe froze, staring off toward the slough. We had not been here before, but he knew exactly where we were. He headed for the slough. Phil and I exchanged glances and took off after him. Within seconds, Freebe dove into the tall grass and weeds at the edge of the slough and came out with the now-dead mallard.

He delivered it to me, but refused to surrender it. All the way back to the vehicle, he alternately walked at heel and trotted around us with the duck held high. In the years we were a team, I never lost a bird. Seemed to me he took pride in that.

The greatest single teaching for me came on a pheasant hunt. It was a huge field, and Phil was working the cover about half a mile away. Freebe and I were in tall canes, maybe eight or nine feet high. Next to the canes was a black, freshly plowed hillside. A large rooster boiled out literally from under my feet. At my shot, he tumbled onto the plow-ed ground 15 or 20 yards in front of me. In the nine or ten seconds it took me to get to where he fell, he was gone. Just pheasant feathers.

When I told Freebe to find the bird, he headed back toward the canes. I knew that couldn't be right, since we had walked from them, and hadn't seen the bird. I was sure he'd run over a hill in the plowed field, so I called the dog back and pointed him over the hill. "Find the bird!" He started toward the canes, again. "No!" I said, "Find the bird". He took one or two steps up the hill, sniffed, and started for the canes. This time I yelled at him. I just couldn't understand how such a smart dog could act so stupid.

He looked at me (actually, he glared at me). Then he trotted the half-mile across the field and started hunting with Phil.

I blew the whistle 'til I was blue in the face, and walked after him. By the time I got within a couple hundred yards, he cautiously came to heel, fully expecting to be punished for the unauthorized absence from his "master." Of course, by this time, I'd begun rethinking my own IQ. As we walked back across the field, I apologized. Freebe, as I recall, sort of shook his head and sighed. We returned to the pile of feathers on the plowed ground.

"Find the bird, Freebe." He just stared at me. "It's OK," I said. "Find the bird." "Please." He took half a step toward the canes. When I didn't speak, he leaped into the canes and came out with the dead rooster, which had somehow run back into the canes as I was stumbling out of them. He gave me the pheasant, and licked my hand.

Christmas seems to be about giving and getting love, and I'm often amazed at how much I have been unconditionally given. Thanks, Freebe. And a merry Christmas to you, wherever you're hunting today.

Photo by C. J. Reynolds

MOURNING DOVES

(September, 1990) Dove season opened this week. For as long as I can remember, dove hunting has inaugurated fall.

Funny how a guy starts thinking when dove season rolls around. I sometimes get flooded with snapshots of feelings or odd moments afield. Visions of stuff like a young kid in the wilderness, rattlesnakes, and happy dogs. And a crystal-clear memory of a water hole and an angry father.

I had to be about nine, I guess, when I decided it was time for a real wilderness experience.

So, after school on a beautiful early fall Friday, I loaded up my old army-surplus, ski-trooper backpack. I threw in a couple spuds, a skillet, matches, bedroll, etc., and wrote my folks a note.

Then I picked up the old single-shot Winchester Model 67 .22 rifle that had belonged to my late uncle Van, and headed for the wilderness--a 100-acre apple orchard next to our place in East Wenatchee, Washington. The doves were in full migration.

At dinner time, I sneaked up on a large dove (well, it seemed large at the time) and made some meat. I fried the dove and a potato over a little apple-wood fire until I couldn't stand it any longer. All I remember about the meal is that I did the whole deal myself, and it was as good as anything I had ever eaten.

At dark, I decided to finish my wilderness adventure in my room. My folks greeted me with hugs as I returned from the wild.

A couple decades later, I was slipping through the trees along Bijou Creek, out of Deer Trail, in eastern Colorado. We were a few hundred feet off Interstate 70. My brother-in-law of the time, Claude Hemsi, was a couple hundred feet away, working up the other edge of the trees. We were bantering back and forth about our shots.

Hunting doves (or anything, really) with Claude was a humbling experience. The guy was a Colorado state trapshooting champ for several years, and he seldom missed. He liked hunting with me, so he avoided pointing out my shortcomings. But really, why would he have to say anything? My shooting spoke eloquently of my inferior genes.

On this particular day, Claude was feeling the force: he WAS the oneness of eye, hand and twelve-gauge.

As he walked over to pick up a downed bird, he was giving me the moment-by-moment description of his incredible, impossible shot...when he stopped in mid-word. Not just stopped, but literally with a word stuck half-way in his throat. It was as if I could hear the middle syllable trying to escape, but frozen at an instant in time.

"Hey," I called, "you OK?" To no response. I started off in his direction. Fast.

A long moment later, I heard one shot. I found him frozen, in mid-stride, hovering over a barbed-wire fence strand. He was white as a sheet.

As he regained his composure, he described--in awesome detail--the terror of crossing a fence and discovering that he was inches away from, and gazing into the beady eyes of, a large, apparently unhappy, rattlesnake. He used his gun barrel to push the snake away, then shot into the sand in front of it in hopes of running it off. All the while, of course, remaining in his one-foot-on-the-ground, one-foot-in-the-air posture. I loved it!

During the too-few years I was allowed to spend with my first Labrador, Freebe The Wonder Dog, we had hundreds of great days together afield. His first dove hunt was one of our best.

The problem with doves is their feathers. The loose feathers leave a pup with a mouthful, even after the bird is handed over to the hunter.

For several minutes after his first retrieves, poor Freebe would sit there going, "ptt.. p-ptt... spttt!" at heel. He was growing increasingly reluctant to go get our doves, and I was becoming impatient. At one point, he brought back a dove and started nuzzling and licking me, getting gooey little wet dove feathers on my arm. I was pretty disgusted, but I remembered something one of the Topeka Retriever Club members had said about this sort of situation. Finally, I stuck my fingers in his mouth and wiped the feathers off his tongue.

All of a sudden, he was eager again! I began to understand "team," and from that day, we were inseparable.

I've learned a lot over dove hunting.

It was over doves, back in East Wenatchee, that I learned a key lesson in hunting ethics and responsibility. I was 13.

Of course, it was dove season. Cousin Tommy Minshall was over from Tacoma, and we decided to go shoot some doves at a waterhole next to a nearby orchard. I grabbed the shotgun and shells, and off we went.

When we returned, we proudly showed my father our two limits of the delicious little birds.

"TWO limits?" The Old Man was not as impressed as I'd figured he would be. "YOU have a license, but Tommy has no license! Licenses are how you put something back, for the birds you get. How will we have doves forever if people cheat?

"Hand me the shotgun, Jimmy. We'll talk about this later."

We did, too.

CHOOSING ANIMAL BUDDIES

(May, 1996) Another beautiful spring day here in Paradise and the agenda item was "hunting dogs." Actually, it was about how one manages to find a good dog. And about dogs' senses of humor. Having once been owned by Freebe the Wonder Dog, I figured I knew a thing or two about both.

Time was, I believed that WE chose our pets and our animal buddies. I even collected several of those "How to Pick a Hunting Dog" articles.

By the time Freebe had been retrieving birds in the Happy Hunting Ground for a couple years, when I could no longer stand being without a dog, I dug out those articles. I looked at pedigree and enthusiasm. I observed how the pups interacted in the litter. And I chose "Buck".

Buck was almost untrainable. If he wanted to walk or hunt in the same direction as you, he'd work with you. If not, he'd just leave. A professional trainer once called him a one-in-a-million lab. I gave him to a farm family. They spent months trying to convince him to not chase trucks. Then, one day he caught one. So much for going by the book.

A year after Buck retrieved that semi, an old friend called. He had new pups. Good pedigrees. Based on all he knew about the parents, and his gut feeling, they would be excellent hunters and companions.

We sat in his back yard talking about dogs and wives and kids and birds and hunting. The pups played and tussled and showed their early retriever instincts. I liked them. I couldn't decide how to choose one...or even if I should. Then one of the pups bounded up and looked me in the eye. He had deep brown intelligent eyes. And a sense of humor, I thought. "Gusto" chose me. It was a pretty happy choice.

One evening, I went to his kennel to bring Gusto in to hang out with me. I was almost out the door, when I remembered that Gusto was gone.

I've had dogs go hunting or retrieving without me, but it was always because I stopped to eat, or couldn't hit anything, or something like that. I'd never just packed my dog off with a buddy who wanted to take him away for a few days. But along comes Jim Erkel, my sometime, longtime elk, deer, antelope, duck, pheasant and quail hunting buddy.

"Hey!" He says, "Let's take off for a few days. Supposed to be lotsa birds this year. For Colorado, anyhow. Let's take ol' Gusto there and go have some fun. We deserve it!" The guy can tug at your heart.

I couldn't get away for another week, at least. Erkel chastised me about not making enough "memory bank" deposits, then said, "Well, how about if I take Gusto myself?"

I wanted to say no. After all, a man's dog is his dog. Gusto might not behave or hunt well, and Jim doesn't really know how to care for a lab, etc. Then I thought, "So what?" Sure, Freebe had been highly trained for field trials and hunting. Gusto, aside from whistle and obedience training (Stop NOW! Sit. Heel. Come.), was left to his natural abilities. So, I said, "Why not? He deserves a break, too."

Erkel had hunted over Gusto, but he'd never handled him. (Funny how we say that: I never felt like I "handled" Freebe, and for sure not Gusto.) Anyway, teaching Jim the whistle was easy. "Wow," he'd say, as he saw how to ask the dog to slow or stop or come back or heel.

I helped load Gusto and his gear. And started thinking about the time I really got Freebe's sense of humor, and his ability to be disgusted.

On a frosty December morning, 1972, Phil Jackson and I were duck hunting (playing hooky from our graduate work) on Lake Perry north of Lawrence, Kansas. The area we were hunting had blinds about two hundred yards apart. Each blind was on a marshy point. The ducks were flying. Memory can be funny, but this is how I remember *that* morning.

Freebe would stay perfectly still in the blind. He'd hear their wings and sometimes see the ducks coming before we did. If we didn't react, he'd whine softly. Only his eyes moved as they circled our decoys. Tense as a bowstring, he'd await our shots, and the command: "Back!"

On that command, he'd become "Freebe the Wonder Dog!" Diving headlong into frigid waters to retrieve our bird, he would joyfully and proudly deliver the fat, brightly colored mallard or wood duck or widgeon to the hand of his clear-eyed and straight-shooting master.

What a life! What a dog! (From his first puppy retrieve, I had the idea Freebe wanted applause or a marching band when he delivered a bird to hand.)

Unfortunately for Wonder Dog, on that day neither Phil nor I could hit the broad side of a barn. The blind to the north had two hunters, but no dog. Every time ducks came even close to their decoy spread, they'd knock at least one down. For an hour, the dog watched us miss. While duck after duck fell into the water in front of the north blind. Another flight came straight into our spread. We missed. Again.

Freebe had the most disgusted look I ever saw on his mug. He walked into the water and swam toward the other blind. One by one, he picked up their ducks and dropped them by their blind. They laughed, thanked and applauded him. When he finished, he swam back, shook himself at the water's edge, and came into our blind. He looked me in the eye for a moment, looked at Phil, and laid down at my feet. Sighing.

Oh, yeah. Gusto did okay with buddy Jim. Jim later swore that when he missed a couple shots, Gusto gave him a really disgusted look.

When it's time again, I guess a dog with the right sense of humor will pick me. Anybody need a stack of "how to" articles on choosing a dog?

Freebe the Wonder Dog   44

PART THREE

WILD WINDS
AND
OTHER ADVENTURES

WILD
WINDS

(October, 1995) About a week ago, I talked with a group of men and women in the Elderhostel Program at Central Washington University. Mostly, they were here to hike and enjoy this ideal time of year in our valley. I'd been invited to spend an hour or so talking about our climate and weather. Figured I'd tell them all I knew, but didn't know what I'd do with the other 55 minutes.

It worked out. We talked a lot about wind. After all, when it comes to the Kittitas Valley's charm, wind is a defining characteristic.

Then, a couple weekends ago, Roger Reynolds and I took the Pearl Street Working Dog, Free Beer & Outdoor Think Tank Benevolent Association to the North Potholes Wildlife Area. With the PSWDFB& OTTBA safely in the canoe, and called to order, Roger proceeded to teach me to paddle like I knew what I was doing. He also demonstrated how to catch a very nice bass. We settled most of the wildlife issues in the state, had a good lunch, paddled back to his rig, and adjourned the meeting. We strapped the canoe down enough for high winds. That wind stuff, again.

Believe me, I know a thing or two about wind.

In early October of '88, I headed into the Red Desert of southwest Wyoming to rest and recreate. The gales there that weekend make our winds look like gentle breezes. I experienced things out there in the desert that I still have a hard time understanding, but what I am about to tell you is all true. I swear it on my editor's grave.

It started out innocently enough. I had this antelope license. An antelope license in the Red Desert is a gift directly from All That Is, since (1) it is tough to draw, (2) the antelope in the desert are very big, and (3) the desert is magic. I was off to make meat.

The Red Desert teems with life: wild horses, antelope, deer, elk, sage hens, eagles, hawks, snakes, lizards and you name it. I knew the first morning that this was going to be a special trip. About 40 miles of clay road into the desert, I stopped to watch a big herd of antelope on a daybreak run. Behind them was a very dense, fast-moving cloud of glowing red dust, and behind the cloud of dust was the rising sun. Through my binoculars I saw, behind the antelope and in that glowing dust, a herd of eight or ten ghost-like wild horses. The antelope, the dust, and the mustangs were all running full-out in the same direction. It was breathtaking. And magic. It was the Red Desert.

The wind and dust were so strong, I opted to spend the weekend near a small seep lake. Right away, I noticed something odd.

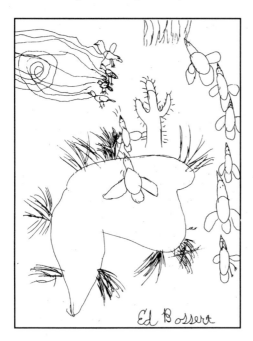

Meadowlarks. Hundreds of them. They were lined up along the far shore. One by one, they walked up the shore into the wild streaking wind. When they got to the head of the lake, they would leap into the air, fold their wings, and blow like rockets to the other end of the little lake. Once they hit the ground they would hunker down and start the trek, single-file, back to the head of the line. One little bugger just kept losing his balance. Tumbling in the wind head over heels, he'd hit the ground bouncing, then shake his head and feathers and stagger back to the line. It was one of the most fun afternoons I ever had.

Streamlined antelope came and went. I didn't recognize the one I was to take, so I just took pictures. At dark, I headed back to my rig.

When I finally struggled back to where I'd left the truck, I realized my foolishness. I'd parked it cross-wise to the wind, on a flat. It was gone. The wind-drifted skid marks led over a rise about 300 yards downwind.

I found it, and managed to get it backed against a hill, facing the wind. All night long the truck gently rocked in that wonderful wind. Dreamt my mother was singing me lullabies. The best night's sleep I ever remember.

The next morning, for the heck of it, I took my fishing gear to the lake, along with my rifle. There had to be some good trout in there.

The wind was incredible. I had to crawl the last few yards to the lake. The birds were at it again (or still), and wild horses moved downwind about half a mile out. A few antelope wandered in and out.

I rigged up a silver and red Dardevle®, cast out into the whitecaps and watched for the splash. The spoon never touched the water! The line was tight in the wind and the spoon was spinning crazily just inches off the water. Suddenly, a trout--a good pound--leaped from the water at the spoon. It missed, but the wind swept it to the bank, where it ripped through some thornbrush and landed on the sand. Before I could react, another nice trout did the same thing. It was incredible! It was all I could do to hold that rod in the wind. My arms were so sore and tired I gave up once there were enough trout in the sand to feed my tribe. I crawled to the trout. They were already dressed! Apparently, the thorns had gutted them as they blew through.

About noon, I finally saw the buck I wanted. He came in a hundred yards upwind. I got as steady as I could in that wind and squeezed the trigger. It was blowing so hard it blew away the sound of the shot. Still, I knew I had meat, because I never miss at that range. But the buck never flinched. Then that 7mm slug came whistling back past my ear.

Eventually, a fat young buck moved into range downwind. I was enveloped in a dense dust cloud, but somehow managed to go home with antelope meat.

Some unusual things happened during that weekend, too, as I recall, but you'd probably not believe them. I do know a thing or two about the wind, however...

THE ELK WHO CALLED ME

(November, 1995) A couple weeks ago, I called Roger McKeel, of the Department of Fish and Wildlife, about the county's deer situation. While he was at it, he also helped me understand the "spikes only" regs for our over-the-counter elk licenses.

The elk part came up at our recent off-Pearl Street wildlife meeting.

We have plenty of elk. The problem has been too few bulls among them. With too few bulls, yearlings (spikes) end up doing the breeding. This extends the rut--the breeding season--nearly into December. This means the calves will be small going into next winter. This makes the problem worse over years. Hunting of spikes is to help protect the older bulls. My concern had been that the pressure on the spikes would remove the lower age class bulls from the population, and ultimately do more damage than good. Turns out that somewhere around 20% of the yearling bulls have branched antlers--and not all the spikes are taken, anyhow. The harvest of older bulls is controlled with permits (limited entry): the number of bulls of all age classes is rising; the rut is dropping back to a bit over a month; and DFW's post-season goal of 15 bulls/100 cows is getting closer. Makes sense.

That settled, the issue on the floor was "strangest elk experiences."

Now, I guess I've spent most of my life exploring the relationships among us humans and those who offer up their physical bodies--their lives--for our sustenance. With elk, I've had a few hard-to-explain experiences.

For example, we were in the White River National Forest of northwestern Colorado. We were out to make elk meat in country I knew well. October, 1981.

Son Tim, buddy Jim Erkel and I were hunting. By first light Sunday morning, I was watching a favorite draw. Nothing was moving.

At about 8:30, I heard several shots from the distance. I was certain that Erkel and his old lever-action rifle had an elk. Every year he took his elk from the same stand. And I could find that stand blindfolded.

By 9:30, nothing was doing and the sky was starting to spit rain and snow. Thinking about the already-slippery and steep jeep trails between us and the highway, I decided to hunt my way quietly over to Erkel, help him pack out his elk, and be out of the canyon by dark.

About 300 yards south of Erkel's stand, I got my bearings. As I said, I could find his stand blindfolded. I knew exactly where I was.

I took maybe five or six steps. I don't really know how to describe the feeling that came over me. I felt suddenly lost... disoriented or confused, maybe. I was almost sick to my stomach--as if I'd badly misjudged something important. I backed up the five or six steps.

Deciding I was too low on the hillside, I headed up. Within 75 yards, I realized I'd been right the first time. I paused and struck off on a straight line to Erkel's stand. In fewer than thirty feet, I was overcome with the "lost" feelings, and almost nauseated. I backed up.

This wasn't my way of being in the woods. I started a conversation with myself, and headed up the hill at an angle. This was ridiculous.

This very same experience repeated itself no fewer than half a dozen times. It was literally as if Erkel was at the hub of a wagon wheel, and I was walking around the rim. Each time I tried to walk down one of the "spokes," I was overcome with that disorientation and nausea.

I came to the edge of a steep draw I knew well. It seemed strange, foreign, but I followed it down until I was certain. I had walked clear around to the north of the stand--the "hub." Disgusted, I took off toward Erkel. It happened AGAIN. It made no sense. Maybe I didn't know this area after all. There was one way to find out.

I followed the steep draw toward the bottom. The timber opened up and, across the bottom of the main valley, I could see our camp. I had walked all the way around! Briskly now, I headed back toward his meadow. It was easy...a "spoke" I could walk. As I stepped out of the aspens at the lower edge of Erkel's meadow, there were three large spruces directly across the meadow from me. Two in front and the third tucked in between and behind them. Laying at the base of the third, almost hidden, was a spike bull. This had to be Jim's elk.

As I approached, I could see that it had not yet been dressed. I looked up at Jim and waved him down, muttering about why he hadn't field dressed his bull. As he walked down the meadow toward me, the bull moved. Startled, I finished the task someone else had started.

It turned out that Erkel hadn't seen the bull move into the trees. He hadn't fired a shot. (We later found out that an old man with a large family group we had taken to calling the "Longmont Mafia" had emptied his rifle at the bull, but had never followed up on his shooting.)

Had I walked into the meadow a few feet up or down from the "spoke" I was on, I would not have seen the elk. Had I met Erkel as I originally intended, we would have returned to camp on a trail from which we would not have seen the dying elk in the spruce trees.

Did the elk somehow offer itself, knowing I'd honor its gift? Did it call me? Was it a hunter's intuition? Imagination? Guidance of God... of Spirit?

I've had a few hard-to-explain elk experiences. Meeting adjourned.

The Rut Race ©1985 Parks Reece

HIGH COUNTRY MAGIC

(September, 1990) Ever have one of those little things that sits way, way back in your mind? ..Like a thought that hasn't been thought in a while? Or, maybe like an urge to do something not done for too long? Something like a piece of you that's been kept under wraps for awhile?

You know what I mean: You get busy with life's obvious things, and let slide the things you really want (or really NEED) to do.

Maybe, these "things" are like moments which define who we are in the world. Things like hunting in country so steep and remote that you can be there alone. You can keep the joy and pain of a gutbusting climb to yourself. You don't have to share the sunset, or the breathtaking crispness of September air at 11,000 feet just as the sun first blazes its light across the high country. You know, moments from way down.

Now and again, you may find a person who shares those moments of the soul. You realize that there may be room in the sunrise for one more.

Anyhow, what got my juices cooking about this was a story I heard last week. I had just dropped off the manuscripts for the next *Walking Whole* brochure and quarterly schedule of my "self-improvement" workshops at Miller Mimeo, in Denver, for printing. The guy who owns the printing outfit is Tom Mann. Tom lives out in Parker, hunts as much as he can, and generally tries to be a responsible citizen. Anyway, I'd said so long to his daughter Staci, and waved to his granddaughter, the two-year old who brings the sunshine in, and was on my way out the door to an OK day of obvious things. Tom hollered from the back of the shop. "Hey, wait a minute... I got a story. You'll appreciate this one!"

Seems that one of the new members in the Denver Chapter of Safari Club International (SCI) drew a permit this year to hunt a bighorn ewe up in the Mount Evans area. Like a lot of us, the guy has dreamed of matching wits with a really huge, old ram, but this year, being on the mountain and connecting with a smart old ewe would be good enough.

Anyhow, he and his buddies spotted a band of sheep wa-a-ay up on the mountain, and headed up to check 'em out--surely there would be an old ewe in the bunch. After busting their humps for hours, the guys arrived to find that the sheep were gone. Of course.

The guy with the license slithered over a windy ridge, to check out another basin. He found himself in the midst of more than a dozen grown rams. Fifty feet away, straight out, was the biggest ram he'd ever seen... and not a ewe in the bunch. Said he'd do it again, just to be there. One of those magic moments.

Since then, I've been sifting through my own magic moments.

Three years ago, this week, I was packing base camp up into some God-blessed country towering over the Blue River. I was coming in the back way, out of Vail, into the Gore Range/Eagle's Nest Wilderness Area. Four days alone, hunting mountain goats, up the Piney River country. The last two miles up seemed like a giant staircase, and I kept prodding myself with thoughts of a great supper by the fire, and not another human in miles. It was worth it.

The next morning, I crawled out of the sack and found two other hunters stumbling through my camp. So... OK, go up. By sunup, I was far enough up Kneeknocker Pass to have the first rays to myself.

Over the four days, I scaled cliffs and scrambled down avalanche chutes. I got overheated and chilled, refreshed, and exhausted. I was scared and exhilarated. I was totally alive: in that way we become alive when we bring some genetic urge from way back in our minds and give it front row in our lives.

Goats were everywhere--big ones, little ones, old ones and young ones. But not the goat I was to receive.

I left my base camp nestled into some tough old scruffy trees at timberline, and returned to civilization to do some obvious stuff.

When I returned to that country a week later, I saw no one else.

On the second day of that trip, I scratched up into a cirque, scoured by some long-gone glacier into the west wall of a straight-up-and-down mountain. I crawled out onto an outcropping, and took a break.

I was debating about finding a way up a cliff to a rockpile I was sure held an old billy, when I felt a chill.

A large goat slowly worked its way down off the cliff, onto an outcropping a couple hundred yards away. From the first moment, I knew this was the goat I was to take. After a short stalk, and one careful shot, I gave thanks and went to work.

I dressed, skinned and quartered the goat, a little nervously perched on the outcropping. I was a hundred feet over more outcroppings.

Now and then, I looked down on Piney lake, some eleven miles down the trail. My 4Runner was waiting patiently down there in the trees, somewhere.

Somehow I got the goat out of that cirque and down to my base camp.

The next morning, I figured out my strategy for getting two 70-pound packs--the goat and camp--back to my truck. I could do it in stages, I figured. Two loads down the two miles of "stairsteps", then a couple long hauls down the Piney River trail to the trailhead. I took a deep breath, and started doing it.

A year later--the late afternoon of that same day--the last three miles with the second load were more than I could do. I knew I couldn't make it. I sat down on a log, exhausted. After a moment, I remembered a taco place a few miles down the road. I shuffled that last three miles with a hot cheese and bean burrito in front of my nose.

Just now, I'm remembering a tough backpack trip that Dr. Joe Zbylski and I took up into the desert mountains of Arizona a couple years back. A really tough trip after desert whitetails, the little Coues deer. We've talked about doing it this year again. I wonder if Dr. Joe is by his phone?

An Occupational Hazard
©1987 Parks Reece

PART FOUR

MENTORS
AND
FRIENDS

Reintroducing the Wolf ©1996 Parks Reece

PARKS REECE

LOOKS
AT
THE
WORLD...

The Crack of Dawn ©1993   Parks Reece

(August, 1995) Chris Colon, (as in ":"), this rag's general manager, looked at me with those questioning puppy eyes. He had just handed me the press release and packet of material from the Roslyn Art Gallery describing this Montana artist, Parks Reece. The gallery planned a show of his work, illustrating his "unusual environmental perception." "I think maybe you might like this guy...got a strange way of looking at words and phrases. Maybe you'll want to write something about him. His stuff is pretty funny. So, what do you think? Hmmm?"

Frankly, at that moment, I did not have much energy for people with normal environmental perceptions. My kids were arriving and this meeting of the PSCG&TTBA was stretching on a bit. Roberts' Rules of Order were being violated right and left, and no one seemed to care.

I took the press package, murmuring something like, "Well, sure, uh... let me think about it," which is something like that word the Kenya Winabe tribe uses which sounds like "yes" but means "I will consider it from now until eternity..." I had no intention of talking to anybody.

Besides, artists--people who make pictures or sculptures or whatever-- are strange people. Like writers. We all like to ask stuff no one else has the courage or simpleminded curiosity to ask. For example, I know a bright sixteen-year old--Stacey--who wants to be a Marine biologist. Now, Stacey is like a daughter to me and I think I understand her okay, but I cannot for the life of me figure out why anyone would plan a career like that knowing that the Armed Forces are being cut back. And what about buffalo wings? They're tiny, and they're probably the only white meat on a half-ton animal. Where's the rest?

Somehow, around lunch time on July 22nd, I stumbled across the press release. I had to go get my mail, anyhow, maybe I could stop and look around. Then there was the free luncheon. Columnists and adjunct professors don't get a lot of free lunches.

I figured I'd look around at this guy's paintings, have a bite to eat and see whether I was supposed to get to know him.

One of the first paintings I saw when I walked into the gallery from the top of the stairs was called *Re-introducing the Wolf.* Against a striking backdrop, here was a silhouetted wolf shaking hands (paws?) with a cowboy. Lined up behind the cowboy were deer, elk, rabbits, buffalo and others. People who know about this stuff have begun to call Parks Reece a "modern mythic surrealist." I have friends who are successful "realists," producing paintings of wildlife ready to walk off the canvas, and at various times I've owned samples of their work. But I don't think I ever looked at a painting and wanted to laugh and cry at the same time, until I saw that wolf being re-introduced.

I wandered around the gallery, trying to balance a plate of free lunch and maintain an air of sophisticated bemusement. Before a painting of a coyote howling at the moon while sitting in a patch of prickly pear cactus, I heard a man tell the artist that he didn't get it: "Why is this one titled *Why the Coyote Howled?*" "Well," patiently replied Mr. Reece, "I was on an antelope hunt with my ten-year-old son. I had stepped in a cactus-- very painful--and that night when we heard the coyotes howling, my son said, `I'll bet he sat on a cactus'."

Antelope hunt? I'd rather hunt antelope than do almost anything. It was a sign. We struck up a conversation and were soon swapping li.. uh, stories, about kids and antelope hunting and cactus spines deeply installed where only a spouse or very good friend would remove them.

We were looking at his work, and chuckling about his view of things like *The Crack of Dawn* (one of my favorites), *Bisontennial, Bear Rappellent, Debait* and *The Legend of Velcrow.* We talked about the fun in looking at words and phrases in ways that others didn't, or couldn't. And there's a way of looking at the whole world which sets some people apart. I once interviewed an 88-year-old woman for "Colorado Reflections," one of my radio projects. She showed me her flower garden. She knelt among some full-flowered daisies, almost in awe...as if she was looking at them for the first time. I asked if they were new. She laughed and said she'd grown them for sixty years. I'll never forget: she looked at those flowers with the fresh eyes of a child and the heart of a woman who understood what love really was. She was joy, she was alive.

I saw that in Parks Reece. And in his work.

Others wanted some of his time, also, but we talked long enough to know we had lots more to talk about. I have a feeling that one day soon our paths will again cross. He's a bit strange. I liked the guy.

If you sometimes see nature in an off-center way; if you have a sense of humor about how we humans do things these days; if you need a chuckle; if you have interest in, or awareness of, wildlife, the outdoors or the issues about which we debate and argue, you've GOT to see this guy's paintings. If you can't find a nearby show of his work, it's probably worth the trip to go see his Murray Hotel studio in Livingston, Montana.

Why the Coyote Howls ©1990 Parks Reece

ICE FISHING, GOLFING AND OTHER INSANE HOBBIES

(April, 1996) Springtime. Everything is greening up. I'm thinking about fishing and wild turkeys and gardening. But, I seem to be passing through one of those "theme" times. You probably experience them, too: those moments in life when, everywhere you turn, people are repeating the same theme. For me, it seems generally to be one of those things I don't want to do...

This week the theme seems to be golfing. Every time I turn around someone is talking about golf lessons (or is actually taking them), trumpeting the merits of a game one can play at any age, or asking me if I play. Thank you: I have no interest in learning the game.

While I did chase white-tailed deer around a golf course once (the deer were reaching "pest" level), I know little about the game. As cousin Ron might say: "I've never seen a 'golf,' although I have found some of their holes and their round, white, dimpled eggs. And I've seen how they crop the grass real close around their holes (which is probably why those guys carry metal clubs). But, honestly, I have never seen a golf and don't see what all the excitement is about."

One of my fathers-in-law once tried to get me to take up the club. Much as I loved the guy, I'd entirely given up on golf years earlier.

When I'm reminded about golfing, I start thinking about ice fishing. And Rick, some years before he scrambled his brains on that motorcycle.

January, 1964. Buddy Rick decided that it was time for us to explore Colorado's ice fishing. It sounded very simple. And cheap, to fit our status as enlisted men at Lowry AFB. This was only a couple weeks after Rick's father argued that we should take up golfing, to gain a bit of sophistication and class. We couldn't understand why he thought we needed more class, but agreed to think about it through the winter.

"Look," Rick said. "All we need is summer stuff we've already got. And, when we find that its as much fun as I know its going to be, we can pick up or make whatever else we need." Summer stuff? "Yeah, lawn chairs, a cooler, that portable barbeque of yours and our fishing gear... and maybe some warm clothes. This is gonna be great!"

I know we caught a few fish--I have the pictures--but I barely recall the "fishing" part of our ice fishing. I remember stuck cars and wildlife and blizzards and drinking coffee in lawn chairs next to a charcoal fire. And laughing at the insanity of watching fishing line disappear into a constantly re-freezing, six-inch, hole in the ice.

Our first trip was to Monument Lake, between Denver and Colorado Springs. Halfway across an unplowed parking lot was a three-foot-high snowdrift. Our "mountain vehicle" was my sturdy 1956 Rambler Wagon. "Just goose it," Rick said. The good news was all the available 4X4s to pull us off that drift. The bad news was they were racing on the lake. We tested our gear in a little cove outside the marked racecourse. We marveled at how the vibration and engine noise kept the hole from re-freezing.

We got good at finding hotspots (just look for other ice fishermen). We grew fond of South Park, known since its discovery for its ground blizzards. On our first winter trip to South Park's Eleven Mile Reservoir, we chose a cove we knew from summer. The sunrise was beautiful: no wind, the sun was out and the whole park sparkled. We cruised down the flat, snow drifted tracks that led to the cove. What we didn't remember from summer was that the old road had dips in it three or four feet deep-- it wasn't supposed to be flat. It all came back to us as we dove into snow blasting over the windshield of the Rambler. Ever the pragmatist, Rick said "Ta hell with it, lets go fishing. Someone is gonna want through here bad enough to pull us out of the way. And if not, one of these other guys will invite us home with him tonight!" We caught lots of trout that day. And, sure enough, someone pulled us out. He even thanked me for breaking most of the way through the dip.

We drove out at the very end of the day's sunshine--at that moment when the light charges things with sort of a magical cast. As we cleared the top of a hill, we saw hundreds of antelope herded-up in the distant snowy pastures below us, along the road. A great chance for photos! I crawled on top of the wagon. Rick was to casually drive through the antelope and I'd get some great shots. I've never been so cold, but I knew it would be worth it! (After all, great photographs require adversity.) My eye was glued to the camera's viewfinder. I could hear Rick laughing as we drew closer to the antelope. He stopped in the middle of them, as they slowly turned into sheep. "Woolly antelope!" He laughed and laughed. As I got down off the top of the wagon, I noticed a rancher staring and shaking his head. And to this day, "woolly antelope" jumps into my mind every time I see a sheep. And I can still hear Rick offering to stop for pictures.

In late February, we headed off to another ice fishing adventure. It was barely light, and there were four or five inches of fresh powder on the ground in Denver. KOA's weather guy told of blowing and drifting conditions and very cold temperatures in South Park. We were drinking coffee, and talking about golf. We agreed that we would learn the game in the spring. It had become obvious that we needed some kind of sanity in our lives. As we turned onto Hampden from Colorado Boulevard, we looked over into the Wellshire Golf Course. There was a foursome, in the cold and the fresh snow, with ORANGE golf balls.

I looked at Rick. He was staring back at me.

"Naahh!"

To this very spring day, I have never swung a golf club.

Enough is enough.

WHO SHAPES US?

(May, 1995) I was digging through a couple boxes the other day. (You know how you just have to sort through that old stuff now and again?) One of my office mates wondered aloud if I was living in the past. I guess I chuckled, but I was thinking something like, "Man, I hope not..there's only two boxes here."

For some reason, I got to thinking about the Old Man. Not long before he left this life for the other side, we were talking at my house in Denver...about hunting and fishing. He asked me about my outdoor mentors. "In particular," he asked, "how'd you get so nuts? Who got you started in the outdoors?" I had to think about that for a moment. I guess I told him I knew he loved the outdoors, and I appreciated all his encouragement, but he was too often too busy for much hunting and fishing when I was a kid. Cousin Ron was important, but I only saw him a couple times a year until we were teenagers. Then I remembered Earl.

Earl English was really the first guy to take me under his wing. He watched over me from the time I was eight or so until I was sixteen and moved from East Wenatchee, Washington, to Yakima. Earl was six or eight years older, and was maybe even crazier than me about outdoor stuff.

After I was grown, he told me that in those early years he felt like I was a little lost puppy chewing on his cuff. Said he never could figure out how he got so attached to me, but I always seemed to have worms and eggs for fishing, or odd 12 gauge shells for birds, so...

Funny how people are. The first time he let me hang around, he was trying to figure out a load for an old .45-70 military rolling-block carbine. Somehow he'd traded for it and was determined to find a way to shoot it. He found some brass and gunpowder, then cast .45 caliber slugs with a mold he picked up somewhere. The lead was from assorted sinkers. What fascinated me, as I look back, was his casual way of testing the loads. He wasn't unsafe or anything--in fact, he was very safety conscious--but it was where he shot. We lived in a neighborhood of homes on 1 to 2 acre lots. Earl's room (the "lab", he called it) was upstairs. He simply leaned across the window sill and blasted the slugs into a target and sand pile down in the yard. The Old Man would have murdered me for that, I knew. I was hooked.

Earl was a very funny guy. He knew everything, and was generally willing to teach me. In spring and fall, we'd fish the Wenatchee River, the Icicle, or the White for salmon or steelhead coming up out of the Columbia. I still remember his way of rigging the salmon egg sacs and hardware, and how he said the fish would talk to each other while admiring his rig. When I was younger, he'd make sure I was in a safe place on the stream. I don't think I ever actually landed a fish on one of our "big river" trips, but it was always exciting. Anyway, being in the presence of such genius and humor was reward enough.

In summer, we'd fish the beaver ponds. That became, over the years, my favorite activity. We would catch a big mess of 6- to 8-inch brookies and race back into town to the smokehouse. The guy at the smokehouse would charge us two-bits or four-bits to smoke-cook the cleaned trout for an hour or so. Then, we'd sit down in the shade and eat them like corn on the cob. Sometimes, we'd save a handful of the trout for our families. I've never eaten anything better. Anywhere.

In fall, we'd hunt doves, then quail and pheasants and ducks. The old man often gave me trouble about how Earl would shoot my shells up, but it seemed a fair trade at the time. I'd say "Lets go hunting!" Earl might say, "I'm out of shells. If you've got shells, I've got gas." And off we'd go. My dad had probably saved a handful of 12-gauge shotgun shells out of each of 30 or 40 different boxes of ammo over the years, so we shot some pretty strange stuff, even for the early 1950s. It didn't matter to us, and we rarely came back skunked.

We had a favorite duck pond. It sat on a cottonwood bench high above the Columbia River, south of Wenatchee. On the cold, windy days of November, the mallards would sit on it by the hundreds. We would sneak up on the pond, then stand up and shoot as the birds rocketed over the trees. Then, we'd sit and wait. Soon they'd be back. To this day, I find few things better on the table than a fat mallard, and those northern grain-fed birds are still the best.

A decade or so ago, I arranged an antelope hunt in Wyoming for Earl and a couple guys he brought with him from Wenatchee. It was, for me, a way of letting him know how much I appreciated the way he looked after and nurtured that "little lost puppy." He was still funny and we had a great hunt, but, of course, we were different people by then. I wrote him a year or so later, and the letter came back "addressee unknown." I haven't located him since. I guess that's okay with me.

I don't think I much want to live in the past. Still, maybe those who shared our paths got us to the present. Maybe this remembering stuff is just about honoring those who helped make us who we are.

Anyhow, I'm back home in Washington again, and even Colorado seems a long way away. I got kids coming who need to learn about beaver ponds and brook trout. And is there anybody around who can smoke-cook a bunch of fresh brookies into summer memories for a new bunch of lost puppies? I need to start looking ahead here...

COUSIN RON AND THE SAGEBRUSH MALLARDS

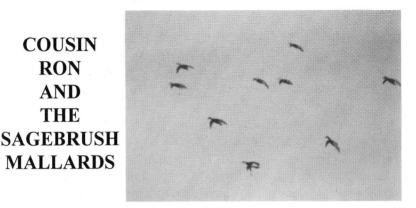

Photo by C. J. Reynolds

(November, 1988) A year ago, cousin Ron Tanquary came to spend a few weeks in our foothills. He came for healing. And to catch up on the 25 or 30 years since we'd spent any time outdoors together.

Ron is probably the best storyteller I've ever known. Our weeks were filled with laughter, outrageous lies and remembrance of growing up in the Yakima and Wenatchee River valleys of Washington State. Even the wildest stories couldn't change how we had been blessed with fantastic fishing and bird hunting.

His visit had a bit of frustration, too. This man--certainly the most complete outdoorsman I've ever known, the guy who taught me to catch a meal of trout in any stream, who taught me to creep to within a couple feet of rabbits and birds when we were six years old--was paralyzed. A boat trailer accident in his driveway triggered a stroke, leaving half his body dysfunctional.

His stories escaped the stroke. And they still had the power to carry me wherever they went.

During our too-few weeks together, Ron rode along on his first antelope hunt. We built crawdad traps, feasted on game, and he improved a bit. He headed northwest--home--as the ducks headed south.

While we waited for his plane, we talked of our escapes from family, and duck hunters hardly bigger than the shotguns they lugged along the edges of the rivers and canals. "Anybody can jump ducks on a slough," he laughed, "but few ever jumped 'em like we did that day in the Wapato country."

I've been watching the ducks this fall. More than I have for years.

Ron is walking a lot, I hear. Stronger, but unable, yet, to carry a shotgun on a sneak down the sloughs. I look forward to hunting ducks with him again, and I still hear his laughter that day in the Wapato country.

It was exactly 30 years ago--1958.

The valleys in eastern Washington can be pretty foggy--REALLY foggy. And way long before light on this particular morning, two teenagers headed toward Wapato to jump mallards off the sloughs. The farther we drove out into the valley, the foggier it got. We were navigating on hunches.

We couldn't see 25 feet, even when we could see through the fogged-up windshield of his old Chevy. Finally, Ron said "Jumping 'em is not gonna work, man. We'll never see 'em in this stuff. I got an idea."

Over the years he'd noticed that the ducks flying between two of the largest preserves and the grainfields where they fed always flew right over a particular hill. It was a sage-covered hill, rising a couple hundred feet above the surrounding valley bottom. Maybe, just maybe, in the dense fog, the mallards would fly LOW over that hill.

Hmm. Now, of course, all we had to do was find that hill. In the dark and in the fog. Somehow, we were guided to the base of the hill.

The air was heavy, as it often is in fall near sea level. There was a damp chill that bit right through our clothes. The walk up the hill warmed us up just enough to really start shivering as we separated on the ridge to wait for daylight.

Right away, we knew we were in for something special. We could hear--and feel--the mallards hurtling over the ridge only yards away, chuckling now and then, as if to locate each other.

It was a once-in-a-lifetime experience. You could hear the mallards' wings, and chuckles, but in the fog you could not see them until they came right over you--full tilt and 30 feet away--like miniature gray "ghost" jets. "Whoooosh", and they were gone. You shot quick or stood there feeling foolish. At that range, it was a clean hit or miss--nothing in between. In maybe 45 minutes it was all over.

We stayed a bit longer, hoping for stragglers. No such luck. We gathered up our few mallards, and, as always, marveled at their striking colors and size. As the fog lifted, we swapped stories and laughed about great shots and amazing misses, and headed down the hill.

We weren't expecting what happened next.

About 50 yards down through the sagebrush, mallards started flushing in front of us!

Apparently, as they came over the hill crest and the ground faded out of sight in the fog, many of them panicked and landed. We were flushing ducks out of the brush everywhere. It was like the best pheasant hunt we could ever imagine--but they were DUCKS!

By the time we reached the car, we had plenty of fat ducks for one trip. And stories for a lifetime. All thanks to Ron's "hunch".

Ron's still the best all-around sportsman I've ever known. And I have this hunch that one season soon we'll be kicking fat mallards off a slough somewhere.

I can't wait.

Photo by C. J. Reynolds

PARTNERS

(July, 1995) Some years ago, I realized that it was easier to replace a good wife than a good hunting, fishing and camping partner.

I remembered this realization during a brief meeting of the PSWDFB &OTTBA. One of our more blunt members asked how many wives I had had. I wasn't sure how to respond, since at least two of them had had me, but I did try to honor the spirit of his question. In the process, I counted up about as many wives as good outdoor partners.

For a time in my life, it got confusing: my third wife--Joan--was also my third really outstanding outdoor partner.

On our first camping/fishing trip, I knew it was gonna be good.

For starters, she never doubted me when I told her I had the heaviest pack. Then, after trying to entice a fat rainbow trout to take a fly (and everything else in her tackle box), she opened the long blade on her Swiss Army Knife. She slowly moved into the stream and impaled our 15-inch dinner. A few years later, pregnant with our first child, she got her first antelope with one shot. You get the idea.

The other two partners were men. Sometimes I still really miss them. I miss that masculine soul-buddy kind of humor and camaraderie and rivalry. And the never-knowing-what-was-coming-next-but-knowing-that-you'd-live-through-it suspense of hunting and fishing trips. One of these partners got his brains scrambled. The other got caught in the middle of one of my divorces.

I met Rick when I landed at Lowry AFB in 1963, after a stint over in Korea. We were both in radio and TV production. It was about as much inside work as we could stand, so evenings and weekends we headed out to ice fishing or whatever else called us.

Rick was a born cowboy. A cowboy from suburban Boston. He bought a Stetson, a pair of boots and a Winchester .270 (his hero was Jack O'Connor). We taught his .270--and ourselves--to hunt antelope. By the time the hat and boots were broken in, he even talked western.

Rick was part of me. If I was thinking thirsty, he'd hand me a cool one. If I was thinking about casting long, he'd cast short. He always took the duck on his side of the blind, and he never shot the pheasant that got up in front of me until I'd emptied my shotgun.

On a deer hunt, we'd separate to work a long hillside. We'd move slowly through the timber for an hour or more--a hundred yards apart--and we'd reach our designated rendezvous within a minute of each other. Firearm or fish hook, safety was never an issue. We just always knew where the other guy was.

In time, Rick became a pretty good dog man, with some excellent German shorthairs. We had the best pheasant hunting Colorado ever offered.

With growing families and increasing responsibilities, we escaped less often. Still, our campfires were special. And he'd still pretend to see a deer or elk on another mountain just to get me over there.

In spring, 1970, I accepted an offer to finish my graduate work at the University of Kansas--KU. We planned a fall reunion in the hills, and talked of his dogs working Kansas birds. Late one night his wife, Elberta, called. Rick had split his helmet in a motorcycle crash. He came home from rehab, but never grew beyond an unmanageable 6-year-old in a man's body. His wife moved the family, and I never found them again. In 1981, he was in my mind for months and I felt that maybe he'd died.

On antelope hunts, I still hear Rick marvel at the speed of the "goats". Now and again I still hear his laughter and tales of the day's hunt across my campfires.

I met Phil at KU. A California boy and a fellow grad student, he was very quiet in the classroom, but in the field he came to life. He was a wonderful storyteller--and some of his stories were probably true.

Phil never got dirty. Or wrinkled or greasy or bloody or any of the other things you go fishing or hunting to get. He'd clean as many fish or birds as I did, but he'd look ready for the office, and I'd be blood and guts from head to toe. He loved it--said I was a born slob.

The guy could shoot. He was a fine wingshot, but exceptional with the rifle. One year we scheduled a fall hunt in Wyoming, but the hunt had to be postponed until Christmas. Great guide that I am, I found the herded-up antelope our second day out...in the middle of a blizzard.

Tough stalking, it was. Finally, between white-outs, laying over a snowdrift, Phil called and made the best shot I've ever seen. He wasn't feeling well, what with the blizzard and altitude, so I dressed the animal and carried it on my shoulders a half-mile to the vehicle.

As I turned to get in, I looked at Phil. I still don't know how, but he was a mess from head to toe! And I looked ready for the office.

The next summer, Phil and I took an antelope scouting trip up into Wyoming. His wife stayed with my about-to-be ex-wife. Haven't seen him since.

Some years ago, I realized that it's easier to replace a good wife than a good hunting, fishing and camping partner.

ABOUT ROY ENTER

(January, 1990) We'd discovered a magical parcel of land out by Elbert, Colorado, south and a bit east of the Denver metro area. Buddy Roy, stockbroker-realtor-rancher-outdoorsman, had helped us find it, but hadn't yet seen it. When I took him out to look it over, he said "Well, if you like being this far out and you can do out here whatever it is that you do, then it's perfect." The next day, he said, "I keep thinking about that land of your kids. I've come to the conclusion it's some of the most beautiful land I've ever seen. Make the guy an offer."

I started laughing. In one of those "flashes" you hear about, I saw pieces of what Roy's shown me. About life, living, and perspective.

I met Roy Enter on the top of a mountain. Near Hourglass Burn up in central Colorado's Tarryall mountains. It was August, 1974. We had bighorn sheep licenses. We were looking for the big rams we both knew lived up in that country.

Canadian "Cousin" Norm Hardy and I were hunkered down in a hollow in some rocks at the top of a ridge in the Tarryalls. We were soaking up the sun, out of the wind, and eating lunch. Norm was facing me. I had taken my hat off and was resting my head back against a boulder. The wind was blowing the tips of my hair around.

Several things happened at once: I felt a chill zip down my spine; Norm's eyes got big as saucers; and I saw the hawk's wing tips on both sides of my face as it frantically changed its mind about digging its talons into, and eating, my scalp.

It was an omen. The evening of that day, I met Roy Enter.

Roy was a stockbroker, not yet far enough from Vietnam that he could really relax in the woods. I was a new assistant professor at the University of Colorado at Denver. Roy walked over to our fire that first night, carrying a flashlight and a loaded .45. We shared a beer and talked 'til very late. As Roy headed back to his camp, Norm said, "That fellow is a bit nuts... we could all be great friends!"

Two weeks later, Norm had returned north and Roy and I were back-packing into a remote stretch of the Kenosha Mountains north and west of the Tarryalls. I was about to get my first lesson in Enter's If-You're-Gonna-Go-Go-First-Class School Of Roughing It.

It was a tough hike in, mostly because I decided to walk up a non-existent trail through a mountainside of blowdowns, while Roy took his chances with a trail he found. Roy got to the high basin first.

When I finally made it--exhausted and more than a bit frustrated--he had a fire going, and offered me a beer as I put down my heavy pack. Or wine, if I preferred. Or maybe a long snort of bourbon? Over a lot of laughter, and that cool beer, I slowly recovered from the shock of someone actually carrying a six-pack, plus wine and bourbon, up a steep mountain.

Then, he smiled and asked if I preferred grilled fresh sirloin steak or hamburger and potatoes for dinner...

A few adventures, and a couple years, later, we were on a fall hunt over in the Sleepy Cat country around Buford. After a divorce, I was madly in love with a sophisticated woman who wasn't sure she approved of hunting, although she was a carnivore. Roy took my winning this fair lady as his personal challenge, and set about designing the meal I would prepare to win her over. We killed several blue grouse during the course of our deer hunt, and we selected the two youngest, and most tender, to be delicately apple roasted to form the meal's centerpiece.

I was carefully instructed as to the wine (two subtle, distinct, brands of Poullie Fuisse), the proper balance of salad and vegetable, and the dessert. The wine was half gone as the birds emerged from the oven, browned to perfection. The woman of my dreams exclaimed, "Oh my God, look at this. These creatures gave their lives just so I could enjoy this meal. Thank you. Thank you." The evening did not end exactly as Roy had promised, but we enjoyed an incredible, intimate meal and lots of laughter.

At some point, we graduated to horses. Our first horse trip into the high country involved at least one horse who was not a happy camper.

After eight days and quite a few miles of impatience, this animal popped his cork a hundred feet from the truck and trailer. By the time he was through, his load was spread over about half an acre. The only unbroken things were a Coleman lantern and a glass bottle of vodka. My backpack and its frame were in pieces no more than six inches in length. It took an hour for me to see the humor in horses, but Roy is still laughing.

He now has several horses. They carry everything peacefully, and the man has become a legendary back-country Dutch-oven cook.

We'll make the offer on the land. Maybe we'll get it and maybe not. Whatever happens, we will live our lives as fully as possible. After all, Roy has shown us time and again what a kick life can be!

THE NORTHWESTERN ART OF HALF-WORM FISHING

(May, 1996) Another beautiful spring day here in Paradise. On my desk are bits of news, tugging at my sense of naturally belonging to the outdoors. Here's a journal article on the connection between feminists and animals. (This one appeals to the aspect of my nature which is ashamed of having been born a man in a patriarchal society.) Then there is the (anti) article about firearms training for Boy Scouts and an anti-hunting argument from USA Today. Maybe next time... Today's task cannot wait.

I choose, rather, to explore a deep geographic concept which's been gnawing at one of the lobes of my brain for many years. It has to do with the regional nature of the fine art of half-worm fishing.

It is my thesis that the art of half-worm fishing is a Northwest tradition. I learned the art at tiny pools up the Little Chumstick, a creek flowing toward Leavenworth, Washington.

Recent communication with my Colorado buddy, Gus Mircos, raised the question of geography. Sadly, some arts--even treasured ones--are not honored in other regions of the country. (Even if they work as well in these new regions as they did in their geographic homeland.)

Gus and I radioed together at Denver's KOA for a time a decade or so ago. We've hunted a few geese and pheasants and caught a few trout, and remain pretty good friends. The man has an elephant-like memory. I'd shown him pictures of our Christmas salmon trip, and talked about our upcoming shrimpfest on Hood Canal. I may have recalled something about the nice brown trout I often caught in southern Colorado's San Luis Valley. After a couple disparaging remarks, Gus reminded me of our first fishing trip. He was not being, as I saw it, a gracious correspondent. Why dredge up old innocent mistakes just to insult a friend in Central Washington? And, in truth, it hadn't really been a mistake...I did what I did on purpose and with great purity of heart..

Try as I might, I've never been able to get excited about fishing with artificial lures and flies. Yes, I've caught walleyes and pike and crappies and bass on spoons and leadheads and plastic. And I've caught trout on Daredevles® and Super Dupers® and flies. Salmon have nailed my trolling rigs. But, to me, real fishing is on a lake with salmon eggs, or fishing the pools and undercut banks of a small stream with my all-time favorite fly, the "Garden Hackle"--the common worm.

As you may know, I spent my kid years in East Wenatchee, hanging out along the Columbia and a lot of smaller streams coming out of the Cascades. I spent weeks with my cousins Judy and Gene Palmquist, who lived up along the Little Chumstick Creek in that long valley out of Leavenworth. In those days, Washington Game and Fish set aside the Little Chumstick for kid fishing--14 or under--and (as it still is today) we didn't need fishing licenses. The creek teemed with little brook trout, and had a fair number of rainbows and an occasional cutthroat up to maybe 13 inches or so. Judy and I often spent all day drowning worms in that creek, usually with one or more of the neighbor kids.

Of course, we never used store-bought worms. We dug them in my aunt's garden. Now, my aunt held worms in great esteem. This was right around 1950--before much use of chemical fertilizers--and she held that worms were the reason her gardens always did well. One result of that was that we never took many worms fishing at a time. We learned to not waste them. In fact, we became adept at knowing just how big a piece of worm was necessary to lure the trout out from under the banks of that little creek. We came to consider a dozen worms enough to easily catch a couple dozen trout, and the kid who could catch three or four trout on one piece of worm was greatly admired.

Since we didn't need fishing licenses, the trout added up to "free" meals. Our families loved fish and game, anyhow, but in those years of tight money, the little trout were considered a great blessing and gift. So the kid who brought home enough trout for a meal--on only a couple worms--was really special. The satisfaction went far beyond a few trout and a meal...we always said we were bringing food back to feed our hungry tribes. It's a deep sensation I have even today, coming home with fish or birds or a deer or elk. I like the feeling.

Now, about that first fishing trip with Gus. I had permission to fish a small trout stream near Rollinsville, above Boulder. Gus promised to teach me and my fourteen-year-old son Tim how to properly fish a stream. Out of deeply-felt gratitude for his generous offer, and for the sheer pleasure of his company, I volunteered to bring the worms.

Confident that Gus truly was a skilled worm fisherman, and wanting to honor him for that, I bought only about one dozen worms. He didn't seem to appreciate the honor. In fact, he made unkind assessments of my parentage, my intellectual abilities, and my ability to parent Tim.

I understood, of course, that he was doing that to help me be a better fisherman and all-around person. Still, I ended up having to teach him the fine art of "half-worm" trout fishing. He was an apt, if highly disgruntled, student. Gus actually ended up catching several very nice trout from the little stream. (A direct result of my tutelage, no doubt.) He was the ONLY one who caught any trout on that trip. Of course. I was too busy tutoring him to fish much.

Clearly, this is of grave geographic importance. In the Rockies,

fishermen like buddy Gus take pride in using WHOLE worms. In the Northwest, we... Well, we... Hmmm. Boy, am I glad Gus is not going to see my shrimp bait.

Debait
©1994 Parks Reece

A TRUCK/A FRIEND

(March, 1990) The guy was a genius. He understood my truck's soul. After having the dealer's mechanics screw up stuff on three tuneups, I quit trying to take it to any place other than Gary's Comprehensive Car Care, in Denver. One of his mechanics said something unexpected, and very wise, once.

"Yeah, it's unusual." He said. We'd been talking about how little work my 4Runner had required during its first 100,000 miles. "I know this seems a little weird," he smiled, "but the longer I work on cars and trucks, the more I see that they sorta take on a relationship with their owner... even the personality sometimes."

"And sometimes it's like they're not willing to let the owner down... they just keep going."

From the time I drove it off the dealer's lot, in January of 1986, I felt a kinship with that truck. Like it was instantly an extension of me--of who I was at that moment, and who I would grow to be as we both piled up miles.

I never named it. Nor did I call it "he" or "she". I did call it "buddy" or "guy" on a couple occasions when we were in conversation about what it needed to keep it going hundreds of miles from home, in some mechanical or weather-related distress. And we always got there.

Now and again, someone would ask about my long-running truck. When I told them what kept it going, they'd often just smile and look away.

We were protected in that truck. I learned about it early on.

A month after we bought it, we packed up the little ones and headed to Phoenix to visit my folks. By evening, in a falling snow between Show Low and Globe, we were coming down a long hill through the trees. Three or four inches of wet snow, in four-wheel drive, at a reasonable speed, I figured. We came around a bend. IMMEDIATELY in front of us were two cars which had collided. Both were crosswise in the road, facing each other. No room to go around, without going over the edge on one side or up onto the cutbank on the other. And no way to stop. Between them was a narrow gap, not wide enough for my rig, but maybe better than the options. The last thing I said before I hit the gap was, "OK truck, I'm sorry, just do the best you can." An instant later, we were on the other side. No impact--not even a touch. There were tears I couldn't stop streaming down my face. I didn't quite get it, and I still don't, but that truck was safety for those in it.

I'd drive 65 miles an hour for 200 miles across the country, put it in 4x4, and scratch another 50 miles to some wild place I was going to hunt or fish, or just hang out. We'd crawl across miles of greasy, wet-clay roads, over and around rock outcroppings, and up steep trails I didn't believe we'd make.

In work or play, I never questioned taking that truck ANYwhere. Over the years, we cruised and crawled through remote deserts at 100 degrees in the shade, and through 20 inches of powder at 20 below zero. We crawled through mudholes up to the doors, and over stuff so rough and jagged I was sure any slip would destroy tires and hoses and gas tank.

When our other cars were acting up, and we just weren't sure we could depend on them, I'd have the family take the truck. I just never doubted that it would bring them back on time and safely.

Two weeks ago, the 4Runner turned over 182,000 miles. I'd done very little more than normal maintenance. The truck had been running on will and love for too long. It was owed some things.

Then came the big snowstorm. And the slushy roads after.

On a Thursday afternoon, I was headed for Conifer, southwest of Denver. At a few minutes before five, I came around a bend to a pile of slush in the middle of the road. I got around the slush, but I caught a wheel in the soft stuff at the side of the road. The truck rolled and flipped, landing upside down.

While I waited for the insurance guy to decide if they'd fix it or buy it, I kept thinking about the truck. 182,000 miles. Nearly as I could figure it, that was more than 5,000 hours of my fanny in the driver's seat. How many close scrapes? Did the truck just get tired...or did I?

How many times did I put the key in the ignition, a long way from home, in desert heat or bitter cold and blowing snow, and KNOW that we were going home? How many times did I sense that the truck loved hunting and fishing and far away adventures as much as I did? And how many times did I just know that it was as much a part of me as my heart and my soul?

The insurance guy called just before I started this. They've decided that it just isn't worth fixing--too much damage and too many miles. The guy was kind enough--like he understood.

Goodbye.

And I can't seem to stop the tears.

PART FIVE

SPAIN

THE
BLACK
GHOSTS
OF
EL CASTANO

Jurassic Pork ©1996 Parks Reece

(February, 1990) There's just something about these February nights. Driving back home last Thursday night, I was struck by the full moon. And the feelings I get on such nights in hill country ever since I was a kid.

I awoke Friday morning thinking about Spain. And about El Castano, the ranch where Joan and I spent a wonderful couple weeks in February, 1986.

For years, I dreamed about hunting Spain. Just something that kept nibbling at me. It started, I think, when I was a kid, reading stories by Robert Ruark and Earnest Hemingway. I wanted so badly to make such a pilgrimage, but how would I ever be able to put it together, much less afford it?

Then, one spring evening in 1985, I found myself at a Ducks Unlimited banquet and auction in Denver. One of the auction items was a fourteen-day hunt for red stag, wild boars and partridge in central Spain, in the wild, brushy hill country south of the ancient, walled city of Toledo. This hunt, along with other items, was donated by Beverly Wunderlich, through her booking agency in metro Denver.

Anyhow, Bev is widely known for putting together really special hunts, and this one had my name stamped all over it. The excursion would be with Cazatur, Ricardo Medem's Spanish hunting/touring organization headquartered in Madrid. The hunt would be centered on his huge estate, El Castano, in the beautiful hill country of Las Sierras. The excitement of winning the bidding and sheer terror about how I was gonna pay for it fought to see who could get through my body first.

Somehow, we scratched together the money to back my high bid. Then we arranged for the kids to stay with Joan's folks, in Chicago. And scheduled the hunt for February of the coming year.

That whole flight over the Atlantic, I was like a little kid.

When we finally landed in Madrid, I felt as if I had come home. Javier Trevino, the young nobleman who would be guide and companion during our hunting and touring, seemed like an old friend.

So, after watching that full moon last Thursday night, I woke up thinking about Spain and Javier. And our two nights of stalking El Guarro--the wild boar--by the light of the full moon. Those were the nights of hunting the amazing "black ghosts" of El Castano.

In Spain, the game belongs to the landowner. When animals are taken by a hunter or harvested by the gamekeepers, the carcasses are refrigerated and then transported and sold to markets throughout Europe. In shops in the villages and towns we visited, and at the various places we stopped for lunch, we found red deer, wild boar, mouflon sheep, fallow deer or partridge readily available.

As we loaded into "El Land Rover" for the drive to the new wheat field where we would first stalk El Guarro, Javier explained that the game-keepers fenced the fields of wheat and barley to keep the wildlife out of them until they matured. Then some of the grain would be harvested, and the rest left to the deer, mouflon sheep and boars. The fences kept out the deer and wild sheep, alright, but the wild boars always found a way to get through.

"There is an old thing we say that speaks of this," he told us. "The game belongs to the mountain and the landowner. But the mountain be-ongs to El Guarro!"

Along the east side of the new wheat field was an ancient stone wall.

Near a small stock pond, where the runoff drained the enclosed field, the boars had pried under the woven wire used to close a break in the stone wall. Along this wall, 50 meters from the hole, we would await the boars.

Silently.

"We have now only to

wait," whispered Javier.

Three hours. Three hours of moonlit silence, rifle resting on that ancient wall, or across my arm....eyes and ears straining for the slightest movement or sound in the moonlight. Over and over, I had the sense of having crouched behind such a wall, weapon in hand, for many nights before. Another time--another life, perhaps? At one particular moment, I looked down to confirm that the rifle resting across my arm hadn't become a peasant-soldier's pike. I found myself remembering the exhilaration of being with brave fellows defending the homeland.

And feeling the terror of knowing the enemy was sneaking up on the other side of our wall.

Then I'd look around. Javier, Joan and Crescencio, the gamekeeper, patiently awaited the boars.

9:20. The nearly-full moon is getting brighter. No boars. I started to move--to stretch. Javier placed a hand to my shoulder, and a finger to his lips. Somehow, several of the wild pigs had slipped noiselessly through the fence. As they scampered across the gravel and rock of the stock dam, the sharp clattering of their hooves rattled the silence. Quickly, and as quietly as possible, I followed Javier to the dam.

I realized I was shaking. Like a dry leaf in a wind. The leather string tying up the brim of my old leather hat was making a sound like a snare drum on my head. I told Javier I didn't think I could shoot from there. He could tell that I could also hardly talk. "It is no matter," he whispered, "first we must be calm..." Silence. Then, on the other side of the dam, only a few meters away, a stone rolled. We could hear, almost feel, the deep breathing of an old boar. When he topped the dam, he would be two meters away. My hat started drumming again.

When the tension seemed unbearable, just when I was sure El Guarro would never move, and maybe was not even there at all, Crescencio touched off a blaze down the wall where he and Joan waited 200 feet away. "Grruwff!" the boar growled, and left. Silently, like a ghost.

Javier was livid. In civilized and respectful, but angry, Spanish, he demanded to know the meaning of the fire. The gamekeeper had seen the boars move off into other parts of the 400-acre wheat field. He had not seen el guarro by us, he just wanted to let us know that the others had moved.

The tension broke when someone started laughing at how serious this "ronda"--this moonlight stalk for El Guarro--could be.

Then, with nary a flashlight between them, four grown people began a stalk through the young wheat sprouting from the moist, soft, black soil of El Castano. Off to find the boars.

10:00 PM. A nearly-full moon almost illuminated our crisp, clear mid-February night.

We were stalking through heavy, rich, black soil. With each step, we would sink into the soft soil between the neatly drilled rows of new wheat. In the moonlight, it was like walking on a solid cloud.

El guarro, the boar, was here somewhere.

We worked up along the stone wall on the north side, ears and eyes open for boars. As we slipped around a patch of moncha brush along the fence, a small basin fell open just ahead of us. Javier stopped, and we crouched. "10, 12, 13 boars, James," he whispered into my ear, "at about 60 meters!"

Finding the boars against that black soil and new dark green wheat was impossible.. Slowly, I began to see something scurrying about.

The forms would grow and shrink, fading in and out. It was amazing! Like black ghosts, somehow--getting larger and smaller--standing, running, and turning broadside or toward or away from us. How could I pick one? Javier was growing impatient. I picked one a bit away from the rest.

Kawhoomp!!! Nothing so totally destroys a quiet, moonlit night as the crashing blaze of a rifle shot.

Suddenly, pigs were everywhere! And we were right in their path. As 25 or 30 boars scrambled within meters of us, Crescencio jumped in front of Joan waving his hat, yelling, "Hi! Yii! ..Haiy!.." Javier pointed at a big boar coming right at us and laughed, "Shoot another if you wish. 300 dollars." He loved la ronda for the boars. As he loved making money for Senor Medem.

Turned out I'd missed, of course. The black ghosts were gone home, and we left, laughing all the way back to our chalet.

We were still laughing and recounting our adventure as we headed back the next evening. "Tonight," Javier told us, "we have a different place in your wheat field, with a very BIG boar, maybe."

We watched and photographed mouflon sheep and fallow deer on our trip across El Castano to the enclosed field. There were clouds, and questions about the moon, as we settled onto a small brushy, rocky island in the field of new wheat.

We were, maybe, 150 meters from a V-shaped break in the stone wall. The tracks of a large boar led to and from the hole under the woven wire that the gamekeepers had stretched across the breach in the wall.

8:45. The clouds thinned. The wind settled. Three more-or-less silent hours. My stomach was not quite able to stop its grumbling, and the old gamekeeper's breathing was clearly audible. Joan and Javier just sat, somehow managing quiet.

It was chilly, but as the moon became brighter and brighter, the excitement of the wait grew.

9:15. We all needed a stretch, but it was now the time of el guarro. The fresh memory of the previous night's stalk made the waiting bearable. Almost. 3 1/2 hours. No boars.

Joan and I are silently asking the boars to come to us. My prayer/request is simple: I ask that the boar we are to receive come to us, and I commit to honor him.

Joan is concentrating on the color of an amethyst stone--a color for warriors--and composing a silent prayer/poem:

"Oh boars, is there one great old warrior
among you? Do send him please.
To one old boar who sees himself a warrior;
please come tonight and give yourself to us.
Give us the honor of your life;
So that we too may be warriors.
We honor you and thank you!"

9:30. Javier and Crescencio are silently comparing notes on something in the night. ...A bush, maybe, along the stone wall. It moves... Maybe. They argue silently.

I see something in Javier's face, and move closer to him. He points. I look. Nothing...

Except one lone bush, a hundred meters or so out. It seems to fade in and out, as I watch it. I lean to Javier. "How many?" I whisper, silently. "One," he whispers back, silently. "Very big."

The "bush" just seems to jump all around in my scope, growing and shrinking. I find myself listening for the drumming on my hat to start, again. I breathe carefully, holding as steadily as possible. Still, the black ghost in the moonlight is changing sizes as it turns and moves. Finally, broadside. The apparition clears; is still long enough to be identified.

For a second time in as many days, the dark and stillness of the night is shattered.

Javier is beside himself. Beating me on the back in the no-longer quiet night. "It's a big one James, I tell you. Is a BIG one! Is a gold-medal boar, by sure!"

Crescencio shook my hand, lit one of his home-rolled cigarettes, and made a poem in honor of the hunter and the magnificent old boar. He did this each time an animal gave itself to a hunter on the ranch--on El Castano. Then, perhaps, he might pass the wineskin for toasting, especially if it was an unusually large or brave quarry, maybe even roll a smoke for the hunter. Tonight he passed the wineskin. And rolled me a smoke.

Moonlit February nights are for remembering: Spain; Javier and our friends at Ricardo Medem's El Castano; ....And the black ghosts, who own the mountains.

The Dreaded Cholesterowl
©1990 Parks Reece

LA PERDIZ
AND
THE
"JUDAS"
PARTRIDGE

(January, 1996) A week ago, Sam and I were doing field work for the PSWDFB&OTTBA. It was important to check on the elk at the Rocky Mountain Elk Foundation's Heart K Ranch at the mouth of the Taneum, as well as our small group of wapiti just outside Ronald.

Anyhow, what got me thinking was a covey of Hungarian--gray--partridge that hang around the farmland east of the Taneum Canyon. I started thinking about Spain, and how much pressure one little caged partridge can put on a man. And how sometimes fate protects us.

A few years back, at a Safari Club Auction, I'd been possessed to bid on a trip to Spain to hunt with an outfit called Cazatur, owned by Ricardo Medem. The hunt would be on El Castano, Ricardo's huge ranch in the hill country, south of Madrid. We paid off my winning bid, somehow, and made travel plans. It would be a great trip with an unforgettable man.

Javier Banon Trevino: a young Spanish nobleman, lawyer, officer, guide and friend. We had completed our hunt for el venado (the red stag) and el quarro (the old wild boar). Javier had shown us the sights and magnificent old cities of the hill country south of Madrid. We had found souvenirs for those who sat kids and pets in the U.S. so that we might have this experience. Two full days left, and I really wanted to do some partridge hunting. I knew our guide was antsy for the field again, too, and I had a feeling he had something up his sleeve.

Because it was February, a driven partridge shoot was not possible. "But," said Javier, "I maybe have a very special treat for you. Rare for a foreign hunter! We will see.." He wouldn't say what he had in mind, but that night he smiled as he told us to be ready to roll early. We would travel to Las Arribas for la perdiz--an adventure with the Spanish red-legged partridge (similar to chukars and huns).

As we drove from the home ranch the next morning, Javier could keep his secret no longer. "Today", he said, "you will experience a most special tradition: 'la caza del perdigon'. This is the hunt with the decoy partridge who sings his song to make the other boys mad."

Javier told us of Rufo, the gamekeeper at Las Arribas, who had two male decoy partridges. One was old and wise, a veteran of many hunts, and the other was young, but with proven bloodlines. Rufo called them simply "el viejo" and "el nuevo". Our friend and guide was insistent that I understand the significance of being invited to be part of this hunt. It was most important that I honor the traditions of "la caza del perdigon" and shoot very carefully, for his reputation was on the line. He had spoken to Rufo of my skill with the firearm and my honor and for the first time Rufo's partridges would sing for a foreigner.

As we careened through the Sierras, I looked at Javier carefully. He seemed serious enough. "Javier...this isn't some sort of snipe hunt is it?" He laughed. "No no. When I was a counselor for the kid camp in Maine a few years ago we did your snipe hunt. Here we do something like that--the kids find wings, antler, or something--it's 'gamusino.' No no this is real. You will see. ..And you don't embarrass me, okay?"

There is a saying as old as partridge hunting which translates roughly to "by the day of Saint Anton each female will be with her mate." We were past that saint's day now, but male partridges were still staking out their turf in the brush. This was the time of the decoy partridge. The caged male partridge will sing to establish his turf rights, thus angering the wild males already there. They will come in to run off the interloper. As Javier explained it, I thought "Judas" partridge was more descriptive, but who am I to mess with tradition?

We met Rufo as we pulled into Las Arribas. He was warm, but a little wary. We met his partridges as he placed them in their cages for our trip to the brushy breeding grounds of their wild challengers.

Once we arrived, Rufo placed the cage with El Viejo in a pocket of brush three or four feet off the ground. Meantime, we settled into a blind about 25 meters away, and Javier completed his instructions.

"You must shoot exactly at the signal. If you shoot at the right time, El Viejo he is puffed up and victorious and REALLY wants a fight now, and sings his challenge, so other males come running to give him all he wants. If you shoot too soon, he feels incomplete--he has not finished insulting his challenger. If you miss, he feels defeated and may not sing for a time. Miss twice and he may not sing for days. Miss three times the shot and El Viejo is devastated...he maybe never sings again. These singing decoys cost hundreds of dollars and use up years of training. You are an honored guest here. Don't miss. And don't shoot El Viejo, or my career with Cazatur and Senor Medem is finished at too young a time. And Rufo will kill me. That would not be good."

El Viejo didn't sing. Nor El Nuevo. And no wild birds came, though we'd seen birds in the area. The cold weather was probably dampening the males' passion, since we heard no wild birds singing either.

Over a wonderful lunch prepared and served by Justa, wife of Rufo, I realized that it was probably for the best. We'd had a great morning with an ancient tradition. Who cares if the birds sing or not?

For some reason, about this time of year, I start thinking about Spain. I long to return to the warmth of the country people of El Castano, and to "la ronda" for the moonlight boars. But I'm still not sure I could again handle the pressure of "la caza del perdigon".

The Hazards of Hunting ©1987 Parks Reece

PART SIX

MY OLD MAN
AND
MY DAD

Anna '96

T
O
T
E
M
S

(April, 1995) Brother raven and his tribe have been swooping over our place in Roslyn lately. It's got me thinking about totems, and totem animals. And totem poles.

I remember the first time I ever really *saw* a totem pole. I couldn't have been more than five years old. Actually, I'm sure that I had seen that pole before--I just hadn't *seen* it, if you know what I mean.

We were going to visit gramma and grampa Minshall in Tacoma. We made the trip over the Cascades, from our home in Wenatchee, Washington, about once every six weeks. I don't remember exactly how much fun the trip was for my folks, what with brother Don throwing up about three-quarters of the way up Old Blewitt Pass. But, for me, it was always a special trip.

The Minshalls weren't really our grandparents, but they gave it their best. "Gramma" was my mother's aunt Ethel. Since my parents' folks were all on the other side, the Minshalls were the closest thing we had.

They loved us like grandparents, and they certainly treated my folks like their own kids. We could call "grampa" whatever we wanted, but Aunt Ethel was a little picky. Family legend held that she had been a wild redhead--a real pistol--until she met grampa. And he always claimed that he never could handle her...but that he had enjoyed a lifetime of fun trying. I was the oldest of three boys, and I was right at five when she laid down the law. "Listen you little twerps," she said. "I'll be your grandmother and I'll spoil you 'cause I love you. You can call me 'grams' or 'gramma', but 'granny' will get you a short stay on this earth. I'll be darned if I'm going to be *ANYbody's* granny! Got it?" We got it.

Anyway, that totem pole was in a small town, outside a store that sold groceries, pop, souvenirs and all the other stuff such stores sold after WWII. It looked a mile high to me. The paint, or pigment, on it was faded and worn, like it was very old. The fierce, protective bird face at the top burned right into the center of my being. Seems to me that the Old Man (who had to be all of 25 or 26 years old, but called himself our "Old Man") said something about it being a sacrilege, being used like that.

As I have come to understand them, totems are the symbols--mostly birds or animals--for a person, clan or a family. To honor the wild relations who brought them good fortune or protection, the native peoples of the Northwest would carve images of them into big (generally cedar) logs a couple feet in diameter and 40 or 50 feet long. After coloring the carved images of bear, wolf, hawk, raven, etc. for the family or individual connected with each totem creature, the pole would be erected before the lodge or home. It seemed the greatest clan totem was on top. The one at the store had a raven on top. Or at least I remember thinking it was a raven.

That was a time of dwindling interest in the Native American cultures of the Pacific Northwest. When the old ones passed to the spirit world, their material belongings--and the ancient hand-carved totem poles that stood guard over the clans and families for generations--often went on the auction block. They sometimes ended up in places like the front of that store... places that even many non-Indians felt were not appropriate. I think my old man felt the poles should be burned to release the spirits of the totem animals with no one left to protect--or something.

Now the Old Man never talked much about totems, and I don't know that he put much stock in them for himself. I do know he had no use for killing anything that didn't provide food--especially ravens, crows, hawks and mountain lions. Grampa occasionally would talk about certain animals or birds that showed him where to hunt. "I don't know that I put much stock in the Indians' 'guide' creatures," he might say, "but I do see certain ones before I get my elk or deer...and where the hell were those 'protectors' when I met Ethel?"

Fairly early on, I found that a couple birds were common companions afield. I remember the "Kruuk kru-u-ck kruk" of the ravens, and the "Hooo hoot!" of the owl about as far back as I can remember being on my own. Seems like they were always nearby when I walked that box canyon at my aunt and uncle's place up the Little Chumstick Creek out of Leavenworth. Always like we were looking around together.

On a hunt for bighorn sheep in central Colorado's Tarryall Mountains a decade or so ago, I sat at first light on top of a rocky outcropping. As the sun first touched the sky, I felt that I was someway filled with everything around me. At virtually that moment, a bull elk bugled in the timber below, and a raven swooped low over my head. As the bugle died in the cliffs and forest, a raven feather settled onto my lap.

On many hunts, over decades, the predawn hoot of brother owl has told me that I would be offered a deer or an elk during the coming hours.

So, with all these ravens, I've been thinking. And reminding myself that, for a long time, I wanted to carve a pole with some of my own wild relations. Probably with a coyote, to remind me of the tricks I play on myself with all my occasionally-foolish humanness. And an owl, a bighorn sheep, a cougar...

And a raven on top.

A Raven Maniac
©1987 Parks Reece

The Old Man and My Dad   99

THE HEIRLOOM

(November, 1995) Funny thing about tools and toys. The Old Man always said that a tool made with quality materials and pride, then handled with skill, could become a toy worth time spent with it. It might become an heirloom, passed on. I guess because he always knew that I preferred being outdoors, he added, "And that goes for a man's hunting and fishing tools, too."

With all the second-hand, hand-me-down hunting and fishing stuff I grew up with in East Wenatchee, Washington, I don't suppose I ever figured I would own an heirloom. But stuff happens: in 1980, my shotgun became one.

My first was a Sears J.C. Higgins bolt-action 12 gauge that belonged to the Old Man. Guess he figured that if he weighted me down enough I wouldn't wander too far to get home for supper. It mostly worked.

At age 14, I apprenticed to R.K. Canvas and Shade in Wenatchee. In addition to making awnings and apple picking bags, the place sold sporting goods and firearms. Part of my deal with owner Ray Koontz was that, after working a full summer, I could buy a beautiful Fox side-by-side double for exactly what Ray had paid for it. The shotgun had been there for years unsold, and "cost" was a great price, even if it would take pretty much what I earned for three months of hard work.

Just as I completed my summer's apprenticeship, Ray died. The other employees backed up my story, but the bereaved widow looked at me like I was 14 or something, and offered to sell me the shotgun at a small discount off its current retail price. I understood, then, why the owner had chosen to die. Disillusioned, I left the canvas business.

Eventually, I did buy a "Fox" double. But in the intervening years, it had become a clumsy, cheap, graceless club made by people with no pride. It wasn't the same...not the shotgun I'd worked so hard to get years earlier. I eventually handed it off to a kid who just wanted a side-by-side double and didn't mind its graceless nature. "Someday," I figured, "I'll own a shotgun crafted by someone who really cares."

In the 1960s, Browning marketed its series of superposed (over and under barrels) shotguns in the U.S. Made in Belgium, these were quality firearms--well-balanced, beautifully finished--and way too dear for a kid studying at the university and working to feed his wife and three kids.

Then, in the *late* 60s, Charles Daly produced his line of over/unders made in Japan. I fell in love with a little 20-gauge in the Superior Field Grade. Every line of the checkering was perfect. The metal to metal fit was superb. The wood fit the metal as if it had grown there. When I closed the hinged action, it felt, and sounded, like closing a bank vault. Solid, made by someone who cared. Fewer bucks than the Browning, but I still couldn't afford it. I put it on layaway.

After a year of payments stolen from lunches and books, I owned the Daly. It went with me to graduate school in Kansas, and on many, many pheasant, quail and duck hunts with Freebe the Wonder Dog. As Freebe became an extension of my joy afield, the Daly became an extension of my arm. Together, the three of us made a lot of tasty bird meat.

When we moved back to Colorado in 1973, my salary at the University of Colorado was pretty low. Low enough, in fact, that during our first winter, we needed some extra cash. I put up the Daly, box and all. When the man held out the money, and I took it, I knew I'd screwed up. I was sick.

I had a nice Remington 870, but as Freebe and fall after fall passed, I missed the feel of that Daly. And God sometimes smiles on fools and the foolish.

One evening I was at a board meeting of the new Rocky Mountain Bighorn Society, and realized that the guy at the other end of the table--Joe Zufall--was the man who'd bought my Daly. Turned out he'd sold the gun to a trader for a very nice profit, and wasn't even sure where the old guy was. He promised to check around. For awhile I was pretty excited, but after a few months of no news, it didn't seem to matter much. I never managed to have the money to buy it back, anyhow.

In 1980, my father went home. My share of his estate was his old German pocket knife, a few of his tools and clothes, his good name and a little over 500 bucks. I got to thinking how he'd admired that Daly.

I called Joe, and we located the gun trader who had bought it years before. From a balcony at a gun show, he pointed the guy out, warned me not to use his name (Joe'd beat him in a deal), and wished me luck.

This man was a crusty old bastard, a horse trader from the git go. I mentioned that I'd heard a rumor that he might have a Daly Superior Field Grade over/under in 20 gauge. In the interrogation, Joe's name slipped out. After a tirade, he calmed down a little. Well maybe he did and maybe he didn't, what would I pay? "400 bucks," I said. No way, this one he had was brand new--still in the box. "600 or forget it!" "Maybe 500." Cash? "Well, if its the one I want, yeh," I said.

He brought it to me at the tailgate of my truck, after I followed him home. I carefully turned it over. On the bottom barrel was a tiny scratch from a Kansas hunt with Freebe. I guess he needed the money: he took the most unreadable check I ever wrote from my shaking hand.

The other day, I was cleaning it up and thinking about fall and birds and Freebe. The Daly has become a toy worth whatever time I spend with it. It's an heirloom, you know. I got it from my Old Man.

BEARS

(September, 1995) I started thinking about black bears last week. One of my favorite animals, really, but I hadn't thought much about them for awhile. I was hoping to drum up a meeting of the PSCG& TTBA at the Tav, one of Ellensburg's premiere watering holes. Failing that, I paid for my own brew and listened to the couple in the booth behind me. They'd apparently been in the woods with a bear.

There's just something about bears. My buddy Bob Hernbrode heads up the Watchable Wildlife Program for the Colorado Division of Wildlife. Bob and I hunt every fall, but we like to think about what people and wild things mean to each other year-round. Bob wrote something for a publication about people and bears that I really like: "People who live in bear country will almost always tell you so. While it is sometimes presented as a warning, it is in reality an effort to describe some ephemeral quality of the land. Most people will never see a bear in their mountains, yet the mere possibility of doing so imparts some vital uncertainty, mystery, danger, need for respect and greater depth to the landscape. We need bears in our mountains."

So. I've been thinking about black bears and a house I helped build. And how the Old Man felt about bears.

I've never killed a bear (in this lifetime). Aside from Yellowstone, I've only seen a handful of wild bears. I really like berry-fed bear meat, but mostly I like being in the woods knowing they're around.

Shortly after the archery elk season opened five or six years ago, I was sitting in the oakbrush on a hillside not far southwest of Denver. The sun was high and I was about to call it a day, when movement at the edge of a big open grassy meadow down below caught my eye. Through my binoculars, I watched a very large, coal-black bear lope across the meadow, disappearing into the oakbrush on the other side. I can still see the way the sun glowed in that bear's coat, and the sort of roly-poly way it ran...so graceful and so awkward all at once.

A couple days later, checking out elk sign on a trail in the same area, I followed the fresh tracks and spoor (that's outdoorperson talk for piles of used chokecherries) of a very big bear.

A week or so later, I was heading up into the hills to teach my evening meditation classes. At a hay meadow in the forest where I often saw elk, I looked off across the hay to the edge of the woods, and saw another bear. This one was a rich, shiny, chocolate-brown color, with the broadest head I've seen on a black bear. I pulled over, grabbed my binoculars, and enjoyed a closeup view of the bear as it sauntered from the trees to the highway.

By the time it reached the road, a number of cars had pulled over to watch, and two guys picking up hay bales in the field got in their truck and closed the doors. The bear milled around in a dip just off the road, executed a 180-degree turn, and loped (that roly-poly way) back to the trees. One last glance over his shoulder and he was gone.

Poor as we were when I was a kid, the folks bought a lot with a burned-out basement in East Wenatchee. The Old Man (probably all of 27 at the time, but he already referred to himself as my "Old Man") worked all day and built all night on "our own" house.

In August of the year we moved in, he and three of our new neighbors went bear hunting, up in some wild berry patches in the Cascades. The bear they got was old and fat. And big...big enough that I understood why they wouldn't let me go along. They divided the meat in quarters.

Somehow our loud, know-it-all neighbor, Barney, ended up with the shiny black hide. I think it had something to do with how he would really appreciate and honor it and how he'd have a rug made.

Anyway, that berry-fattened bear was as fine on the table as anything I've ever eaten. One afternoon after the hunt, Barney wandered into our little kitchen while mom was pulling a bear roast out of the oven. "Smells real good, Dorothy, what is that you got there?" She gave him a taste. He smacked his lips. "Why, it's the bear you boys got, of course," she said. Barney turned pale, stammered "Thanks," and left.

Barney had nailed the bear hide up high on his old beat-up barn, and had convinced the neighbor men that bear meat wasn't fit to eat--that the Huckabays were poor white trash that would eat about anything. They had buried the other three quarters. The Old Man was very much not pleased.

As Barney explained how this must be a real unusual bear, the men dug up the carcass, scrubbed it off ("30 minutes of that SOB under a hose," was how one wife put it) and maybe learned a bit about sacred agreements made with those who give up their flesh for our sustenance.

Before I was 16, the old man and I, along with a bit of help from my kid brothers, built on to our house, tripling its size. It was beautiful, especially my room, which I had designed, built and painted under my father's guidance.

By then, the peaches and cherries were about established on the acreage, Barney was drinking more, and my parents were in trouble. They split the sheets, money from the house, and their three sons.

I don't remember much about moving. Mom and a couple of us boys were off to Yakima. I remember walking one last time across the fields where I'd cut my teeth on pheasants, quail, cottontails, doves and ducks.

And I remember that tattered hide on Barney's weathered old barn.

Bear Rapellant ©1985 Parks Reece

DIFFERENT PRIORITIES

(December, 1995) Under revised rules, relaxing the strict agenda requirements of most of our meetings, the tentatively-named PSWDFB &OTTBA came to order. We quickly lapsed into discussions of our relationships with parents and outdoor mentors. We'd all fought with them over priorities time and again, but, we agreed, eventually we began to understand. And our seemingly-insurmountable differences in priorities didn't matter much.

One of my ex-fathers-in-law passed on a couple years ago. He was one of my all-time favorite people--I even named my youngest son (the caboose on the Huckabay train) after him. And he loved the outdoors.

Edward generally liked my stories, but he took exception to one of the early ones in my Colorado newspaper column. Like many of them, that one was about priorities. As I recall, in that particular column, I was encouraging people to put time outdoors building memories near the top of their priority lists...and work somewhere near the bottom.

Anyhow, Edward's problem was that, as the superintendent of a school district, he was the one who ended up dealing with getting the job done when some guy took off hunting or fishing instead of working. I always rationalized MY skipping out on work by making sure my classes were covered. I'm sure it was a conflict for Edward--he talked about how he envied them at times--but he had priorities to keep.

One of my great treats was to hear Edward talk about his father and how he grew up loving to be outside. He was a pretty good philosopher--like all real outdoor people. After he passed on, I started thinking about how I came to the decisions I had made about my own father. And I got to thinking about him and his priorities.

The Old Man lost his father when he was eleven years old. He finished the fifth grade and took on responsibility for helping his mother keep his kid sister fed and in school. This was during the Great Depression, and I guess he learned early on about the value of having and honoring a job. And having a home. Somewhere in there, he forgot how to have fun. And that made it real hard to get him to come play.

He seemed to take life pretty seriously, and I think that I decided at an early age that the Old Man didn't really like to hunt and fish.

I even concluded at one point, when I was about seven I guess, that I'd never learn to hunt with him as a father. He had just taken away my Daisy® BB gun, and blistered my butt, for shooting a sparrow. As I recall, I'd made a long stalk and a successful shot on that little bird, and I was very proud of remembering my Indian training. On the other hand, as the Old Man pointed out between swats, I'd forgotten Rule Number 1: "We don't kill birds and animals that we don't intend to eat."

Eventually, I figured out that he deeply loved the time he spent afield, but just let work priorities push hunting and fishing down his list. Somehow, when we went up to Leavenworth to see his sister Evy, and her family, he found time to teach me how to catch trout in Little Chumstick Creek. One day, when I was twelve, I finally saw how deeply it affected him to have to choose work and chores over hunting.

It was a beautiful early-November Saturday. After work and on weekends, for several years, he'd been building onto our small house. Somehow, he and mom had scratched together money to buy this place with a burned-out basement next to an orchard in East Wenatchee, .

For quite a time, we had lived in the capped-off basement, and the little house he built over it. Now he'd added on a bit to the house, and winter was nibbling at our butts as we were nailing down the *real* shingle roofing over the weathered tarpaper. Pheasant season was open, but he hadn't been out yet.

Sometime in the morning, a rooster pheasant started calling from the apple orchard a couple hundred yards away. Each time that old cock would crow his pheasant challenge, the Old Man would stop tacking down shingles for a moment.

I'd never seen him look like that--like something very deep and far away was tugging at his very being. He'd tack another shingle down, and when the bird would cackle again, he'd hang his head for a moment. I could sense a terrible struggle inside him.

Finally, he looked at me. Almost painfully. He handed me his nail pouch and hammer. "Wait here," he said, and slid over to the ladder and climbed down off the roof. Moments later, I heard the front door close and watched him walk toward that orchard. He was loading our old

Sears J.C. Higgins bolt-action 12-gauge.

I heard the cackle, and one shot, as that old rooster flushed. My mother walked out into the back yard. The Old Man said, "Thanks, Dorothy..." as he handed her the bird and the shotgun. He climbed back onto the roof. He tied on his nail pouch, asked for shingles, and started tacking them down on his new roof. He was smiling.

Years later, he'd start planning his outdoor trips with us a year or more in advance. Whether it was a salmon fishing trip to Ilwaco, Washington, deer in Colorado or antelope in Wyoming, he didn't want anything to get in the way. He'd learned to play, but still managed to honor his job.

I just do things how I do them--and sometimes I even let work get in the way. I have a better understanding of why others do what they do. Somehow, it doesn't matter if we don't all have the same priorities.

ANTELOPE ARE SPECIAL

(October, 1989) There's something magic about antelope hunting. I've never quite been able to put my finger on it, but it somehow transcends all my other hunting.

This year, I was again invited to come play at the Geesen Ranch One-Shot Antelope Hunt at Agate--Colorado's only one-shot antelope hunt. This is the hunt's third year and my third time to take part.

Funny things happen to people when they become part of an event where ammo counts. If a hunter misses the first shot, or takes more than one shot to get an antelope, then the two-person team is disqualified. (They can still get their antelope, but they drop out of competition.) The winning team gets bragging rights, a round of applause, and their names on the frame of a beautiful wood-inlaid picture of two antelope bucks created by R.C. Cherry, of Pitkin, down in Gunnison country. Sportsmanship is the rule of the day: the hunters become very careful about the shots they take.

My partner, John Eaton of the *Denver Post*, took the first antelope of the hunt. After a well-executed stalk, he got his buck with one shot at 8:30 AM. 45 minutes later, HIS partner made an unbelievable clean miss on a shot at a doe, thus destroying the 1989 chances for the Eaton/Huckabay team to be memorialized on that picture frame.

The team of General Dale Tabor, of Lowry AFB, and Roger Whatley, of Westminster, was first to complete. They had their buck and doe with one shot each, before noon, to win this year's accolades. These sportsmen, and the other 22 who take part, make this Colorado One-Shot special.

Our Saturday evening banquet was a laptop affair of prime beef and Anasazi beans prepared by Dick Geesen and Gary Schlomer, of the Colorado School of Trades.

We then saluted the 15 hunters who took antelope that day. In honor of them and the antelope, Papa Bear Whitmore--one of America's top survival educators, and a member of a Sioux clan--led a ceremony of offering and thanksgiving at the end of the evening.

I got an early start the second morning. Several handicapped hunters would join us, and I wanted to be ready to interview them and get photos for a magazine article. First, I had an appointment to meet an antelope.

During Papa Bear's ceremony the previous evening, I'd had a sense of just where I was to be this morning. It was important that I be there as the first light of the sun streaked the rolling hills of the north ranch.

I parked my truck some distance from where I felt I would meet the antelope.

As I walked the half-mile or so, staying down off the skyline, I had a deep sense that I had done this a hundred times or more. Maybe in this life, maybe not, I had watched the sun push the shadows from the low ridges, knowing that I would crawl through and around the cactus, with the sun on the back of my neck. The white and tan antelope would just shine in the first rays of the sun.

At one point in the stalk up the last hill, I half expected to turn and see my stepdad, Ray, beside me. Until only a few years ago, we shared an annual fall hunt in Wyoming. So many times we were given our antelope at the moment of first or last sun, and so much he enjoyed those stalks at the "shining time" for the antelope.

The antelope were browsing in the sun, on the far side of the draw, just where I expected them. I bellied over the ridge, moved off a cactus, said my prayer asking to know which of these I was to receive, and squeezed the trigger.

On the walk back to the truck, after the prayer of thanks and the dressing of the carcass, my mind was flooded. There was an understanding of why I love the antelope hunt so much....why this rolling country, under the brilliant red and orange sky of rising or setting sun, seems to soothe and invite as my blood stirs with the first crisp mornings of fall.

In this life, I came to Colorado courtesy of my Uncle Sam's Air Force Moving & Transfer, and there was an early connection with this Geesen Ranch.

Rick Doell and I landed at Lowry Air Force Base at about the same time--summer of 1963. We immediately struck up an outdoor relationship, and this Geesen Ranch was where, through the 60s, Rick and I learned to hunt antelope--where we learned the meaning of "hunting partners."

On Geesen property, my two brothers and I, and our father, were last together on a hunt--early 1970s. The Old Man took a young buck, which he later barbecued over an open pit to feed our extended family in Wenatchee, Washington. On that hunt, he couldn't walk half a mile, and in too few years after that he didn't have to walk anymore.

I had forgotten about this place for more than a decade. Then, I somehow ended up being invited to come play in this Colorado One-Shot. And here I was again.

I got my pictures, and my interviews, with the handicapped hunters who were making their own memories and magic. I packed to head for home, and thanked Dick Geesen for creating this weekend each year. "Aw, hell," he said, "I don't do anything. It's fun!" Yeah. It sure is.

A Chance Encounter ©1985 Parks Reece

HEROES AND THE MEANING OF LIFE

(February, 1991) "Oh, hell, son..it's just been a working man's life. Nothing special..."

Robert L. Huckabay--my father, the Old Man--and I were sitting on the patio of my house in Denver. He'd driven from his home in Wenatchee, Washington, to see kids and friends. It was a mild summer morning in 1979. He'd suffered through several heart malfunctions over the years, and this time together was special.

Anyhow, we were talking about life.

Specifically, we were talking about HIS life.

We'd always been real straight with each other, but on this particular morning, any remaining barriers were kicked over. We talked about food, women, sex, relationships, children, fishing, hunting, camping, firearms, farming, the depression, WWII and anything else that came up. I had just asked him what he figured his life had been about.

"...And I don't know that it had to be 'about' anything except living. I always tried to be honest with people, and help out wherever I could. Sometimes it worked out. Sometimes I got my butt kicked. I worked at whatever I could, so that we'd have what we needed. We got by. Maybe my life has just been about all of us on the lake camping and fishing. Our picnics and swimming at Lake Chelan. I look around--I see how pretty it all is--and I feel like I'm part of it...like somehow I belonged here with the earth things.

"So, I always figured we should fish, and hunt, and gather as much of our food as we could, and then let God know we were grateful for it.

"Anyhow, I reckon it's just been my life....I'm glad you and me got to share it." He took my hand. Didn't seem like there was much else to be asked or said. I think we both knew that this was our last face-to-face.

Six months later, after commenting to one of our stepsisters about the beauty of the day, my Old Man took his journey to the other side.

One of the biggest blessings of my life is that my heroes haven't left me suddenly. I've had--and taken--the opportunity to be complete with each of them.

My uncle Kenneth Davis--the man who spent every day of WWII as a guest of the Japanese in China--was one of those personal heroes. He loved being alone in the woods or fields, being one-on-one with a pheasant, a squirrel, or a deer. Maybe that got him through all those years as a POW. During our last visit, I really got that he saw a oneness to all life. It seemed to me that the way he treated and loved the people in his life came from wisdom gained in hours--and a lifetime--of hunting and fishing. I miss him a lot. And we shared what we needed to share.

Last week I was in Arizona. I had enough good reasons to be there, but most important was spending time with my mother and Ray--my dad--at their winter "snowbird" home in Apache Junction. I loved it. We laughed and joked and spent several days just being together.

I finished a bunch of questions I'd been wanting to ask my mother about her family and about stuff going on when I was a kid. We talked about her health, and dad's, and everybody who's dying and about when it's their turn.

On a leisurely walk through the desert, I told dad how I missed those annual hunting and fishing trips we had done for so long. He shared his intense frustration about not being able to handle the hills--or even rolling countryside--after his open heart surgeries. Then he talked about how little he could do anymore, but how much he was still loving being with his friends and family.

I asked him what he figured life was about. A small covey of quail skittered off into the cactus in front of us.

He stopped. "I dunno... But look at those little beautiful quail....just feel that wind in your face. And can't you taste the elk roast mother's fixing for dinner? Maybe it's just about LIFE!"

Runaway Imagination ©1996 Parks Reece

PART SEVEN

FAMILY MARCHES TO ITS OWN BEAT

Beyond The Shadow Of A Doubt ©1989   Parks Reece

KID

C
A
M
P
I
N
G

(June, 1995) It was an off-Pearl Street meeting of the Pearl Street Working Dog, Free Beer & Outdoor Think Tank Benevolent Association (PSWDFB& OTTBA). We had been talking about the beginning of the summer outdoor season, and the joys of getting kids into the woods. Michelle mentioned ticks--and pulling several of them off a kid and a friend over the Memorial Day weekend. The question on the floor was, "What makes YOUR skin crawl?"

Allen Sullivan, soon to be establishing the Corvallis Chapter of the PSWDFB&OTTBA, said, "The tiniest whiff of ___'s perfume." While we agreed with him, it was quickly moved, seconded and passed to not deal with crawling skin not directly related to children in the outdoors.

For a time, we were all a bit preoccupied trying to find the ticks we could feel crawling all over us. Pretty obvious that the mere mention of ticks did the trick for most of us.

Of course, we all had tick stories. Most were related to the innate rudeness of these critters burrowing into places that many of us keep secret even from ourselves. Too, there was the obligatory story of the tick swollen to a dime's size with some poor fisherman's blood.

We all talk about it, but have you ever actually seen a case of tick fever? Rocky Mountain or otherwise? It'll make your skin crawl...

We were doing a combination camping, fishing and field trial trip. Freebe the Wonder Dog--in between trips through the weeds and brush with one or another kid on his back--was making points toward the year's retriever trophy. We were in central Kansas. It was June of 1971 or '72. Tick season.

I don't remember much about the trip, but I'll never forget the weeks afterward. Tim was six or seven. Of course, we checked the kids for ticks after our trip. We found a couple, removed them, and didn't think much about it. A few days later, Tim came down with aches, fever, and stiffness. The tick we missed had chewed up a place the size of my little fingernail on the top of the kid's head. We treated the fever medically, but his head pulled clear down onto his right shoulder. It took nearly two months for the stiffness to leave his neck--for his head to return to its normal position. Ticks.

Edward '96

"So what about trying to fish when you got a bunch of kids about to finish breakfast?" One of our guests smiled and said, "My husband used to say the thought of that made his skin crawl."

Back before I had any offspring, a bride and I spent some time camping in Yellowstone. I vividly recall a morning on Yellowstone Lake in July. I felt totally alive, the colors in the morning sun were deep and rich, and the air seemed to flow through every aspect of my being. I stood at the edge of that clear, cold lake, spinning for cutthroat trout, knowing that if this was my last morning on earth, it would be okay. I was even catching a few 14 and 15 inch cutts.

Down the beach from me was another man, also fishing. Looking back, I'd say he was a little younger than I am now--a bit older than most men with young kids. He commented about the morning and how badly he needed to be fishing again, and nervously rigged his gear for a first cast. Then I understood his nervousness. Down the trail behind him came a woman and two little girls six or seven years old--not a lot younger than my Tena and Anna. It was all over. This guy would get them rigged, and while they were casting, he'd turn to his own rod. One time he even got so far as to squat down next to his rod as a fish played with his bait. Over and over, cries of frustration over tangled lines, hooked kid or tree limbs, or lost bait, drew him away from his own fishing. I remember thinking, "No thanks."

As our PSWDFB&OTTBA meeting broke, someone threw one more into the hat. "Okay! What about mosquitos on a beaver pond so thick that little kids are a mass of red bites and welts in about five minutes?"

Enough, already! Tena, Anna and Edward (the last three of my tribe) will be here this week, and I had promised them the woods. I was about ready to change my mind.

By the time I got back to my desk, I began to remember the *rest* of it.

Tim is a father now. He still loves the outdoors, has little memory of his paralyzed neck, and can't wait to get his son into the woods.

That guy at Yellowstone Lake? I remember his wife hugging him, offering to take his girls away so he could relax and fish. He kinda shook his head. "No. Thanks... I need to relax, yeah, but what I REALLY need is you guys." Then he took apart his gear and got serious about teaching his kids to fish. Last time I saw him, He was grinning ear to ear, helping the littlest one unhook a trout.

Mosquitos? Hmmm.. Try these: Tim, Nicole and Michelle, all under six, by our old tent, covered head to toe with mosquito welts, mud and grins; and four-year-old Tim, miserable from mosquito bites, but with a triumphant grin holding his first few beaver-pond trout. And I have other pictures of two of *this* week's arrivals in the Red Desert, next to an old, sweet-water, mosquito-infested spring: holding hands and

joyfully examining spring's wild flowers-- they're covered with bites.

Ticks & mosquitos? Hand me the Deet. A few tangled lines? I can hardly wait.

CHOOSING
FAMILY

(April, 1995) I've been making summer plans for the last of my offspring, who are coming up to play soon. And thinking about family and the outdoors and outdoor buddies and choices. Life seems more and more to me to be about round after round of my choices--and I'm starting to see family the same way.

We often adopt our outdoor buddies as family. Then we greet them as "brother", "sister", "cousin" or whatever, and introduce them around that way. Sometimes the rest of the family adopts them, too.

Phil Jackson, now professing at Oregon State, was one of the best hunting and fishing guys I ever played with. I once introduced him to my mother as the son she hadn't met yet. Damned if he didn't quickly become her favorite son. So much for choosing family.

There's a flip side to this. When and how does family get chosen as outdoor buddies? These kids coming up from Colorado are about where they can drop their guise of being my small responsibilities and become my partners in the outdoors. This summer, here in the Washington Cascades, I know we'll figure it out: I've looked at this flip side before.

A few years back, I was sprawled in a boat on Anderson Ranch Reservoir in Idaho. It was quiet--middle of the day--and for the first time I REALLY saw who was in the boat with me. There were three of us-- dad and me and my first-born son. We all have different last names.

Raymond's been my dad since I was 17. Born in 1911, he grew up in the hill country of southwestern Idaho. They lived on their "chickens" (grouse), fish, deer, rabbits and anything else earth provided. As I heard it, this Spaniard drank hard and backed down from no one in his youth. When I met him, he was a skilled mechanic laboring for Garrett Truck Lines and madly in love with my mother. I was struck by the deep love and peace of him. And his endless jokes and easy laughter.

The man loved to fish and hunt. In earlier days, he may have strayed an inch or so beyond the letter of the law to feed his family. And maybe he still jokes about the need to do his deer hunting at night, when its safe from all the other hunters. For all his stories, I've never known a more honest man.

He showed me quiet strength, humor, and love. I taught him to hunt antelope. Seemed like a fair trade.

We hunted antelope together over quite a few years. We fished and hunted other critters, too, of course, but the antelope hunts were special. Dad is a patient man...and tough. One time he crawled on his belly for more than half a mile--over a couple hours--to get a clean shot at a nice buck. Naturally, he got the buck with one shot, but for a week he was picking Wyoming cactus spines out of his chest and belly. My antelope hunting is done without him these days. And I miss our hunts.

James is my first-born. His mother and I were just kids, really, and I reckon you can guess the rest of that story. When James was about six, he asked me to let his stepfather adopt him. I signed the papers.

We stayed in touch--more or less. Over the years, I often thought of him growing up fishing and hunting on that farmland in southern Idaho. The kids from my second family knew about James, and we all figured that someday we'd reconnect with him. A few years back, one of my now-grown daughters tracked him down in Baton Rouge, Louisiana, where he'd been teaching youngsters how to keep customers coming back to a big chain of fast-food restaurants. He and his wife were heading back to Idaho, and they stayed with us for a time. We planned some outings.

This young man loves to fish and hunt, and is making sure his kids learn their outdoor heritage, too. All of this not far from those rolling hills where dad found his role in Nature. Seems to be about right.

Well, anyway, here we were. I'd returned to Idaho to visit for a time with family I didn't see often enough. James got to talking about the 20-inch kokanees he'd been taking from Anderson Ranch Reservoir, and how they always seemed to be striking when he went fishing. And how they seemed to be firmer and tastier than any kokanee he could remember in years. (Ever notice how subtle people can be when luring you into a fishing boat or hunting camp?) We'd been flailing the trout streams pretty heavily. When dad showed interest in maybe doing a little lake fishing, I bit.

So, early on this morning, we were on the lake diligently trolling for those hefty kokes. Everything was perfect. A beautiful day, the right lures, plenty of drinks and food, and a smooth, slow series of trips up and down the length of Anderson Ranch just the right distance out from the bank. We talked. We sat quietly watching the rhythmic bobbing of the rod tips as the pop gear was pulled through the still water. We talked about what had been and is and might someday be. True old family stories and some stories that might have had some truth in them, somewhere. Three generations of family and outdoor buddies who CHOSE to be together.

Did we catch any fish? I can't seem to recall. It just doesn't seem important.

Fishing The Yellowstone ©1990 Parks Reece

SALMON

(April, 1995) "Hey Dad," Tim whispered in my ear, "isn't this unfair if we know we're going to take their money?" The subject of ten-year-old Tim's concern was a pool my brother and father were creating to add a little spice to our more-or-less annual salmon fishing charter. We were at Ilwaco, Washington, not far north of the mouth of the Columbia River. Eleven of us--all family--would kick in three bucks apiece. One buck each for the one catching the day's biggest salmon, the first salmon, and the most salmon. We had warned them. "Yep," I nodded to Tim. "It's probably unfair." I smiled and put our six dollars in the pot.

Of all our fishing trips, this one, in August of 1975, takes the cake. It was the last one my father--the "Old Man"--attended, and the last salmon trip where all three of us brothers were in attendance. We'd gathered in Wenatchee--me and brother Don from Colorado, brother Jerry from Boise--and we'd all brought our tribes. We headed for Ilwaco.

We always caught salmon, but one of the real highlights of our trips to the coast was EATING salmon. Every restaurant and cafe up and down the road featured fresh salmon for lunch and dinner, and many of them even featured breakfast salmon treats. The price was always reasonable, and I never reached the saturation point on eating salmon.

In a very real way, we had grown up on salmon. As kids, we almost lived on it at times. I always thought it was soul food. We spent most of our school years in East Wenatchee, in Central Washington along the Columbia River. The old man worked at about whatever he could find, eventually landing a permanent job with Douglas County's Road Department. 'Til I was at least pushing my teens, though, he worked construction on various dams. Good pay and long hours, followed by months of no work, no money and lots of beans and spuds from the irrigated lands of the Columbia Basin.

Anyway, what that had to do with salmon was this: one of the things they were building on Rock Island Dam was the fish ladder, a steep set of "steps" through which the salmon would theoretically swim and leap to get around the dam. During the salmon runs up the Columbia, and while they were in various stages of building the fish ladders, numbers of salmon would jump out of the ladders and land on the ground. When that happened, the workers were allowed to take them home to mama and the kids. We ate lots of salmon.

One of my all-time favorite stories of faith and salmon has to do with one of those fish ladders. At various times in the construction process, the carpenters or other workers would be laid off for a time. During the building of Rock Island, "Shortie" Engles, one of my dad's best buddies, ended up being out of work for weeks more than expected. He and his wife had nine or ten kids, and things were getting tough. Shortie fretted and looked for whatever work he could find, but there wasn't much in the early 1950s. They were devout Catholics, but Shortie's faith was wavering. His wife (who I remember through my kid eyes had a beautiful, round, peaceful, sort of "cherubic" face) would just smile and hug him. He told my dad that she reminded him over and over that their needs were always met. "The Lord always provides," she would say.

Shortie was finally called back to work. On this particular day, he was still a couple days from grocery money, and they were down to eating only homemade bread. Dad shared his lunch with Shortie, and tried to cheer his proud, but bowed, buddy. As they were heading back to work, walking along the fish ladder, a huge salmon splashed over the temporary wall of the fish ladder and landed literally at Shortie's feet. Dad said Shortie stood there for a minute, wet and stunned, staring at the 40 pound fish flopping on the ground. Then he looked around to see if anyone else was going to claim it, picked it up, said "The Lord always provides!" And took it to his truck.

I thought about this salmon fishing stuff a few years ago. I was living in the Denver area, and came across a newspaper story about the cost and availability of fresh salmon up here in the Northwest. Seems that the Japanese had become so enamored of salmon that buyers were meeting the boats as they returned with their catches. They were bidding so high for the relatively limited fish that even the people on the coast couldn't afford them. For the first time, restaurants were not offering fresh salmon on their menus. When they did offer it, it was very expensive. As it might have been expensive in Colorado. Or

Kansas. Seems significant, somehow. The Old Man would not have been happy.

Now, of course, we don't have to worry about the Japanese buying the salmon off the boats. We can worry about whether there will be salmon to feed our souls. Or who might win the right to catch the last wild one. The papers and other media are full of the story. So, since I came home to the Northwest, I've been thinking again about salmon.

I remember how much the Old Man loved that work--that dam building. "Good, honest, man's work," he called it. I wonder what he'd think now. Now that we're beginning to understand the true costs of taming a wild, living river. He was an honorable man. I often wonder what he'd think.

Well, anyway, about that 1975 fishing trip. My brothers and dad did fairly well, and the nephews, nieces and wives all managed to catch a salmon. Tim caught both the first and the largest salmon of the day, and I caught the most. As we split the whole pool, Tim said "Boy, you'd think they'd learn... They ALWAYS hafta have a pot! They're gonna wanna play poker tonight to get even, too, I betcha."

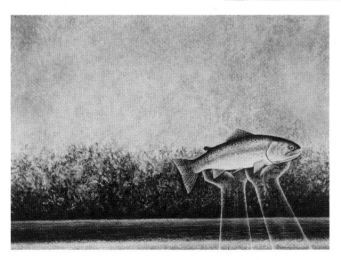

The Gift ©1988 Parks Reece

TRADITIONS AND THE MARCH OF TIME

Tena8'97

(October, 1990) It's been an interesting year. Several things have passed through my experience lately. They've been stirring thoughts about traditions that aren't always recognized while they're being set into family patterns. And about how time marches along even when we like things just the way they've been, thank you. Seems to be one of those years.

At the end of September, I spent a few days in Grand Junction, here in Colorado, in "Adobe School." I went to learn what I needed to know to make the transition from building with sticks (which I've done a bit) to building with mud (which I intend to do in the spring). The school was terrific--there's a magic to adobe and real solar design that transcends any home I've ever experienced. Anyhow, the important thing, here, is that I stopped at an orchard to pick up some apples.

I grew up in apple country, in Washington state, and a lot of my early deer hunting was done in and around the apple orchards of Wenatchee. For me, apple harvest and deer harvest are joyfully intertwined, and I felt an old, sweet anticipation of fall as I stood in that orchard and paid the woman for the apples and the freshly-pressed cider.

The apples came home to the basement until we were ready to use them.

This fall's antelope, elk and deer seasons rolled by. As usual, the carcasses came into the kitchen and onto the table and counters. As our young daughters, Tena and Anna, pointed out, they "got littler and littler and disappeared into the freezer--even the yukky parts!" Two-year-old Edward ("Taco Eddie" he calls himself this week) would climb to the table and exclaim, "Gotum antgope! Gotta deer! Meat, meat," as Joan and I processed our winter's meat. There's a rhythm to life and family, and it always seems sweetest in the fall.

One morning during the deer season, I made a run to Denver. (From Elbert to Denver is just fifty-some-odd miles, but seems like a whole lifetime.) On the radio, the topic of conversation was family stability and traditions. The host and his guest talked about how children learn (or decide) that a place or a family or a situation is safe. They discussed the role of "mobile" traditions--those the family takes with it wherever it goes--in helping kids feel secure. I thought about traditions, but ours didn't seem all that much, really.

When the young buck deer I got a couple weeks ago was all in the freezer, we had to move--the house we were renting had sold. Down the block into another fresh start on the way, ultimately, to our adobe on the timbered hill. A bit unsettling for the kids, of course, and for their parents.

It seemed to me the whole family settled down a little after I whipped up my world-famous "breaded game cutlets, with skin-on mashed potatoes and special pan gravy" one evening. Still, we weren't quite there.

In the moving furor, the remainder of the Grand Junction apples were almost lost amid all the stuff piled up in the basement. A few days ago we got them up into our new (to us) kitchen, found the paring knives, and set about making our famous unsweetened chunky applesauce.

I was filling a couple large kettles with apple chunks, as Joan herded the two littlest kids toward bed. "Abbosauch?" Taco Eddie asked, his hands full of apple pieces. "Yup," said Tena," they're going to put it in jars for us to eat for breakfast and stuff. It's going to be a good winter!"

Got me thinking about this "traditions" stuff. Ours seem to be mostly outdoor-related. Or, maybe it is just this time of year.

Funny thing about them, anyway. The kids grow up with them, and, by the time they're into their 20s, they're already talking about certain hunts and certain places with the kind of nostalgia I thought was for old folks. Or at least for us folks who are "older"... It's scary.

My "grownups"--the big kids, as opposed to the ones still at home--grew up during the years my dad Ray (actually my stepdad, but my DAD) and I spent a couple weeks every year making meat in Colorado and Wyoming. Tim was the oldest, then Nicole and Michelle. Ultimately, the hunters were Tim and Michelle, but Nicole, too, was part of the hunts we did every year.

For a good twelve or fifteen years, every fall, the folks would arrive from Idaho around the last of September.

We'd head out for three or four good days of antelope hunting in the country out of Lusk, Wyoming, or on the Chase Ranch at Medicine Bow. We'd make our antelope meat, explore old towns, collect some rocks and just generally make memories.

As Tim or Michelle showed interest, they'd come along on our stalks and forays after the prairie goats. Each, at 14, began hunting antelope.

After the Wyoming hunts, we'd head home to Colorado. We'd prepare the meat for winter meals--big packages for our growing gang, and small ones for the folks' winter in Arizona. The kids took a full part in this work, too.

Then, the next weekend, we'd head for Montrose, in southwestern Colorado. On the way, we'd meet our good friends the Bottomlys and their kids, and head out to make deer and elk meat. Some years we'd make lots of meat, and other years we would not, but we always had a glorious time and made fond memories.

The kids would miss a bit more school and have another weekend of wildness and adventure. Again, each, in turn, would be tutored in the fine art of making meat.

We'd return home and prepare our new supply of the winter's meat. That done, we'd sit for a day or so--have a good whiskey or a cheap beer, tell a story or two--then pack the folks off to their Arizona winter.

From time to time, a special antelope hunt hit on buddy Roy Enter's ranch in southern Colorado's San Luis valley. The ranch holds a large number of antelope, with a good number of large bucks. Drawing a license to hunt the bucks there took anywhere from two to five years of applying.

Each kid, in time, drew a license. Roy would make it a big deal, with special meals, a little homegrown ceremony and lots of good hunting stories in the ranchhouse the night before the hunt began.

Tim took a beautiful buck there when his number came up. When Michelle finally drew a license for the unit which included the ranch, she blew a shot at the biggest antelope buck I'd ever seen in Colorado. She only smiled---maybe just a little tight-lipped---when she told her grandad about it. Then she said, "Wait until next time."

A few (but still too many) years ago, Dad's energy started waning a little bit. He could still walk his three miles on fairly level ground, but he couldn't handle the hills anymore. I miss his jokes about our stalks and missed shots and I miss... Well, you get the idea. Who could replace him?

So, why am I surprised when a grownup kid says, "Let's go deer hunting in Montrose, again!" Or, "Ya know, dad, I'm really starting to miss our old fall antelope trips to Wyoming."

When I finish this, I'll pull together the gear for a hunting trip. Seems Michelle--after another four years wait--finally drew that "wait until next time" buck antelope license for Roy's ranch.

Steady guy Tony is coming, too. He seems like a good man. Probably make an okay son-in-law one of these days.

I am starting to understand life's progression, I guess. I see it's my turn, now, to be the Old Man.

It's scary, but not likely to stop or slow down.

And I think it's going to be OK.

Order Form

Fax orders: (509) 962-1996

Telephone Orders: Toll Free (800) 221-9631
                              (During West Coast business hours)

Postal orders: **Reecer Creek Publishing**
                 300 North Pearl Street
                 Ellensburg, WA 98926

Please send _____ copies of **WILD WINDS** @ $9.95 USA to:

Name:_____

Address: _____

City: _____ State: ____ Zip: _____ - _____

Telephone: (_____)_____

Book order worksheet:
(Number of copies X $9.95) $_____

Sales tax:
(add 7.7% for books to WA addresses)   _____

Shipping and Handling:
($3.00 first book; $2.00 each additional book)   _____

Total this order   _____

Please send your check or money order for the total to:
        Reecer Creek Publishing
        300 North Pearl Street
        Ellensburg, WA 98926

        Phone: (509) 962-1192